DEAD MAN'S DANCER

by Tom Brennan

Epicenter Press Inc.
Alaska Book Adventures™

Epicenter Press is a regional press publishing nonfiction books about the arts, history, environment, and diverse cultures and lifestyles of Alaska and the Pacific Northwest.

For more information, visit www.EpicenterPress.com.

Text copyright © 2015 by Tom Brennan

All rights reserved. No part of this publication may be reproduced, stored in a retrieval system, or transmitted in any form by any means, electronic, mechanical, photocopying, recording, or otherwise, without the prior written permission of the publisher. Permission is given for brief excerpts to be published with book reviews in newspapers, magazines, newsletters, catalogs, and online publications.

Library of Congress Control Number: 2015933967

ISBN: 978-1-935347-16-3

Printed in the United States of America

Cover images © LukaTDB - Fotolia.com and Rozaliya - Fotolia.com.

Cover design Shorebird Creative, www.shorebird-creative.com.

Interior graphic design by Polly Walter

CONTENTS

CHAPTER 1	Mechele - 2006	1
CHAPTER 2	Man in the Red Coat - 1996	6
CHAPTER 3	The Investigation	12
CHAPTER 4	The Dancer from New Orleans	15
CHAPTER 5	The Traveling Salesman	20
CHAPTER 6	The New Jersey Steelworker	23
CHAPTER 7	The Tennessee Taxidermist	29
CHAPTER 8	The Barrow Boyfriend	32
CHAPTER 9	An Engaging Woman	35
CHAPTER 10	The Last Month	38
CHAPTER 11	Dad Leppink Visits	41
CHAPTER 12	The Letter	44
CHAPTER 13	The Interviews	47
CHAPTER 14	After Alaska	52
CHAPTER 15	The Cold Case Unit	57
CHAPTER 16	The Arrests	63
CHAPTER 17	The Carlin Trial Opens	65
CHAPTER 18	Email	75
CHAPTER 19	A Wedding Present	78
CHAPTER 20	When Kent Met Mechele	82
CHAPTER 21	Amateur Sleuthing	89
CHAPTER 22	The Wedding Gown	93
CHAPTER 23	'Let's Just Elope'	98
CHAPTER 24	The Witnesses	105
CHAPTER 25	Her Trial	108
CHAPTER 26	Two in Prison	120
CHAPTER 27	99 Years	122
CHAPTER 28	Spring Creek	129
CHAPTER 29	The Appeal	132
CHAPTER 30	So Who Shot Kent Leppink?	137

CHAPTER 1
Mechele - 2006

Mrs. Linehan had a wild side. But, her neighbors never knew. Mechele Linehan was the doctor's wife, a community activist and the mother of a young girl, a good citizen. She loved birds and animals, sometimes rescuing stray pets and posting Lost Dog signs around her suburban neighborhood of Olympia until an owner showed up. She worked for several years as a compliance analyst for the Washington State Executive Ethics Board, the agency charged with enforcement of ethics laws governing Washington state employees.

Mechele's husband Colin was a civilian physician with a family practice at nearby Madigan Army Medical Center. Mechele and Colin were preparing to go into business together with a medical day spa offering Botox treatments, laser hair removal, facials and massages.

Mechele was then an attractive 33-year-old woman who was well-liked by her neighbors, co-workers and fellow volunteers. She had raven-black hair, a model's chiseled face, an impressive figure, and a warm personality that played an important role in her success both in the Olympia community and–as the world would later learn–in her past years as an exotic dancer. Colin was a handsome 35-year-old with dark hair, the cautious reserve of a professional physician, and the

2 Dead Man's Dancer

enthusiasm of a man who loves his wife. They were living the good life on Washington's scenic Olympic Peninsula 60 miles from Seattle.

Then on October 4 of 2006, two Olympia police officers showed up at the Linehan door, looking for Mechele. A grand jury in Alaska had indicted her on charges that she murdered a man there ten years earlier. Colin told the officers that his wife was not at home. The officers told Colin he had one hour to produce her. "We could do this in a small way, or in a big way," one officer said, a suggestion that they were prepared to pursue her and make a high-profile arrest if necessary.

Within an hour, Mechele, Colin, and a lawyer showed up at Olympia police headquarters. She was arrested and placed aboard an Anchorage-bound plane a few hours later. Her arrest seemed to close a 10-year-old murder case. Mrs. Linehan was returning to the city where she was once known as Mechele Hughes, hottest dancer at The Great Alaska Bush Company, Alaska's most notorious topless joint.

Colin flew to Anchorage a few days later and tried to see Mechele at the Anchorage Correctional Complex, where she was being held pending arraignment. He took a taxi from the airport and learned, on arrival at the Anchorage jail, that Mechele had been moved to the state's Hiland Mountain Correctional Center in Eagle River.

Rich Gawrys, a bail bondsman now retired, recalls encountering the young doctor at the Anchorage jail and was struck by how devastated Colin seemed by what was happening to his wife. Gawrys offered to drive the doctor out to the Hiland Mountain facility and waited while Colin was reunited with Mechele.

The Linehans' Olympia neighbors were shocked by the charges against Mechele. Few, if any, knew about her past as a stripper or the hard-edged life she lived in Alaska. "She's a great gal," one neighbor told a reporter. "She is one of the sweetest people I know. I don't think I've ever been so shocked in my whole life."

Neither Mechele nor Colin Linehan was taken entirely by surprise when the charges were filed. Both were aware of a letter Kent Leppink wrote to his parents shortly before he was shot and killed on a forest trail in Alaska. The letter named Mechele and two men he said should be considered prime suspects if he were killed. The shadow of Kent's death in 1996 had been hanging over their heads since they first met in college a few years later. Dr. Linehan said his wife told him about her time in Anchorage early in their relationship, and he would say about it only that "It's a complicated case."

One of the odder things about the case was that all three of the men involved–Kent Leppink and the two he named as suspects–had been Mechele's fiancés.

The case drew international media attention from the beginning. The involvement of an attractive ex-stripper turned suburban doctor's wife, a million-dollar insurance policy, Kent Leppink's accusatory "letter from the grave," and her betrothal to three men, made it irresistible to the crime-writers and broadcasters of the world.

Mechele's family and friends in Olympia stuck by her and told anyone who would listen—and many reporters did—that such a beautiful woman, devoted mother, and dedicated community volunteer could not have committed such a heinous crime.

The Linehans' well-to-do neighborhood in Olympia was abuzz with gossip. Though there was nothing innately wrong with Mechele's previous line of work, it was certainly an unusual profession for a suburban doctor's wife. As the details of the case emerged, the public learned that the murder occurred just months after Mechele quit topless dancing to attend college.

4 Dead Man's Dancer

John Carlin III, one of Mechele's former fiancés, was at home in New Jersey when he got word that Alaska State Troopers were looking for him. To avoid being confronted by police in front of his wife, Carlin flew back to Anchorage and turned himself in at Trooper headquarters. There, he was immediately recognized; Carlin was short, stocky, and bald with a red beard. He had a deceptively pudgy look but was actually quite strong.

Mechele was released on bail a few weeks after her arrest and was allowed to return home wearing an electronic ankle bracelet that monitored her movements. Carlin remained in the Anchorage jail pending his trial, scheduled for the following March 7.

Police claimed the murder was committed in hopes of collecting on the million-dollar insurance policy. The victim, Kent Leppink, was a 36-year-old commercial fisherman whose body was found on a trail south of Anchorage in early May, 1996. A tall, balding man, Leppink had a full beard and the muscular physique of a man who pulls fishing nets for a living.

Kent had been one of three men who had given Mechele an engagement ring and considered himself her fiancé. The three lovers had been painfully aware of each other and seemed to remain friends under an uneasy truce, each trying to win her heart for himself.

The case frustrated Alaska State Troopers for years, especially because of the letter Kent wrote to his parents saying he might be killed. If he died under suspicious circumstances, he wrote, police should look to Mechele and her other two fiancés as his likely killers. The letter was mailed just a week before his bullet-riddled body was found on Alaska's Kenai Peninsula. Though there was plenty of reason for suspicion about who killed Kent and why, including both the letter and the existence of the insurance policy on Kent's life, police were unable to find enough direct evidence to make arrests, despite a thorough investigation in the months following the murder.

Also puzzling was a note the detectives found in Kent Leppink's car parked in front of John Carlin's home. It had been written by Carlin and appeared to suggest that he had purchased a cabin in Hope and invited Mechele to use it. He said that he fixed the cabin roof and cleaned the fireplace. "You guys enjoy your stay."

Mechele had scrawled across it, "Great! Please don't let anyone know where we're at ... Love you and thanks again."

The investigators concluded that there was no cabin and the note was a hoax by Carlin and Mechele to make Kent think she was there while she was actually traveling with someone else.

Kent Leppink's murder remained unsolved with sporadic investigation[1] until 2005, when it was assigned to a team of retired Alaska police detectives working on contract to Alaska State Troopers as a Cold Case Unit. Troopers used a federal grant designated to hire officers with years of experience to review old unsolved cases. The hope was that the cold cases could be broken by seasoned detectives using state-of-the-art investigative techniques and scientific advances that were unavailable at the time of the crimes.

---

[1] Investigation in the intervening years consisted of periodic attempts to interview John Carlin IV, teenage son of the prime suspect, John Carlin III. Those attempts were thwarted by the elder Carlin and his family.

CHAPTER 2
Man in the Red Coat - 1996

Spring is a bright and promising time in Alaska, and Mike Gephardt and Morris Morgan were happy to get out of their Cooper Landing office on a Thursday morning in early May. They were spending a day driving across the Kenai Peninsula, a beautiful mountain-ringed place splashed with creeks and icy clear rivers. Gephardt was area foreman for Chugach Electric, the regional power supplier, and Morgan was his partner. They were in Gephardt's utility truck, checking the transmission grid. The winter had been hard, the kind that kept maintenance crews busy for months after the snow melted, and the time was at hand to look for storm damage or problems in the making.

The utility's field equipment looked good; the supervisors found little damage before they turned onto the 17-mile road to Hope, a small town amid spruce, birch and willow trees on Cook Inlet's eastern shore. When they reached Mile 11 just before 10:30, Gephardt pulled the truck into a turnoff and bounced it up a rocky incline. Two electric meters at an old communications site would tell them if there was trouble in the grid–broken lines or damaged equipment, anything that might threaten the system. Gephardt's job was to keep the power on for the entire northern Kenai, and he hoped for a quick stop.

Gephardt scanned the overhead lines and the cleared swaths

Dead Man's Dancer   7

beneath them. All looked well—except for a bright patch of red on the power line trail. Probably gear a repair crew lost off their truck. Picking up after other people was a nuisance, but if he didn't do it nobody would. He pushed the truck door open and headed up the path.

Keeping to the frozen right edge of the trail, away from the soft mud, he hurried up the slope. As he drew near, Gephardt could see the red was a jacket worn by a man lying on the ground. He hoped it was a hiker napping in the spring sun, though somehow he knew it wasn't. He yelled, "Hello." No answer. He yelled again—and again. A few steps closer Gephardt could see it was a man on his back, mouth agape, one side of his ashen face smashed open and bloody. The guy was dead.

Gephardt was momentarily unnerved, but he had police reserve training and knew what to do. Several bullet casings were scattered on the ground; the man had been shot—murdered. This was a crime scene, one unlike any he'd seen before, and he'd better try to preserve it despite the rapidly thawing ground. Gephardt wondered if the killer might still be nearby, then turned and headed back down the trail, carefully putting each foot into one of the tracks left by his own boots on the way up. Beside him on the opposite edge of the trail he could see the dead man's footprints and another set of fading tracks leading away from the body. They appeared to be made by someone wearing medium-size Vibram-soled shoes.

Seeing Morris climbing to meet him and starting yet another set of footprints, Gephardt shouted, "Don't come up here! We have a body." He waved his partner back to the truck, climbed in beside him, and dialed 911. The call rang through to the Anchorage emergency operator, who transferred it to the Soldotna Detachment of Alaska State Troopers. The Trooper office was more than 90 miles from the shooting scene, which was near the edge of the detachment's vast patrol area, so the two utility workers settled down to wait, nervously guarding the approach to the crime scene.

The closest available officer was Trooper Rodney Pilch at the one-man post in Crown Point, 24 miles north of Seward. Other troopers climbed into cruisers and raced toward the scene from Girdwood, a ski resort on the opposite shore of Knik Arm, and the Soldotna Detachment office. The first to arrive was Pilch, who pulled in behind Gephardt's truck about 50 minutes after the dispatch call.

Gephardt told the Trooper what he'd seen and pointed to the body, showing him where he had noticed the Vibram-soled tracks coming down from the murder scene. Pilch noted an indistinct set of tire tracks in the turnout and climbed cautiously up the trail, keeping his own feet in Gephardt's tracks. He could see Gephardt's still-fresh footprints and those of Morris at the base of the slope, as well as those of the victim, but the trail seemed otherwise little marked. Pilch's mind was focused on the body on the trail above him; if there were Vibram tracks leading away from the body, he didn't see them.

Pilch circled the corpse carefully. The victim had a chest wound, a massive hole in his face, and a line of dried blood coming from the left ear. A wallet and checkbook protruded from his right pants pocket. Pilch wriggled them out and checked the driver's license photo against the dead man's face. The body was that of Kent Leppink, 36, and the license said he lived at an address in South Anchorage. Two names were printed on the checks, Kent Leppink and Mechele Hughes, with a different address, a house in Wasilla, about sixty miles north of Anchorage.

In another pocket, Pilch found a set of keys with a Dodge Omni logo tag. The turnout had been empty when the power company inspectors arrived, so the victim apparently arrived in a vehicle that was driven away, perhaps by whoever shot him.

Dead Man's Dancer   9

The man's pocket also contained a completed life insurance form, the kind used to change beneficiaries.

Pilch inspected the three shell casings, which appeared to be from a .44 magnum handgun, a large-caliber weapon carried by some Alaskan outdoorsmen for protection against bears. He pulled sheets from a pad of yellow accident-report forms and used them as markers to flag the spent cartridges for the detectives who would investigate the case. After identifying the victim, his job was to secure the scene and, as best he could, preserve evidence for the investigating team.

The first detectives to respond were Trooper Investigator Ron Belden from Soldotna, who was then northbound in a cruiser, and his supervisor, Sergeant Steve DeHart, who had been called at home and told that Belden was on his way to an apparent murder on the Hope Cutoff. DeHart had sped to his office, got a quick briefing, grabbed a stash of equipment, and took off in the detachment's crime-scene van. DeHart would be the senior officer and lead investigator, so he went to work while still en route, using radio and cell phone to issue orders on the fly.

Motorists on the Kenai Peninsula that morning saw flashing police lights in their rear-view mirrors, glanced at their speedometers and slowed reflexively, moving over to give the fast-moving police cars lots of room. When the troopers blew on past, the drivers breathed easier, happy that their small sins were apparently not a priority that day.

At the crime scene, a few locals, including Hope's postal deliverywoman, stopped and tried to find out what was going on. They were waved off by troopers standing guard at the turnoff entry.

The arriving detectives did their own inspections, photographing the body and the surrounding scene, including a set of indistinct footprints on the melting trail, the ones Mike

Gephardt thought came from Vibram soles. The tread pattern on the footprints had deteriorated further in the thawing mud, so the investigators decided to skip casting, which would be unlikely to provide anything useful. They took close-up photographs, which would at least help determine the size of the suspect's boots. They interviewed Gephardt and Morris, took their contact information, and sent the power company workers on their way.

DeHart became crime scene manager in charge of a growing team of officers working on the hill and at the turnout entrance and others dealing with the case remotely. Troopers at online computers in Anchorage and Soldotna were compiling everything available on the dead man. While those at the crime scene tried to figure out how Kent Leppink died—what he was doing and where he was standing when the bullets struck—others were sketching out the picture of who he was.

First Sgt. Michael Stickler, deputy commander of the Soldotna Detachment, arrived at 1:45 p.m. and did his own inspection of the scene. Stickler had an extensive background in firearms and noted that, because the empty .44 casings were scattered on the ground, the bullets were almost certainly fired from a Desert Eagle semi-automatic pistol. A revolver would have retained the spent shells until the shooter removed them from the weapon manually. A semi-automatic flips them out and away from the gun as each shot is fired. The only semi-automatic pistol that comes in .44 magnum caliber is the Israeli-made Desert Eagle.

The scattered shells also said something about the shooter. The killer didn't stop to pick up the spent brass, leaving useful evidence behind. Among other things, the scattered shells suggested the murderer was either inexperienced with firearms, careless, or in a big hurry.

About 4:30 p.m., the remains of the dead hiker were zipped into a black vinyl body bag. Those who lifted it could tell that

Dead Man's Dancer

the corpse was in full rigor mortis, suggesting it had been there for a while, well before the two power company men happened by. The officers carried the bag down to a waiting medical examiner's transport and sent it off to the Anchorage morgue. Some troopers remained at the turnoff until day faded to dusk, then headed home to write up their reports and get started on what was already looking like a long investigation.

When Kent Leppink's remains reached the medical examiner's lab in Anchorage, they were X-rayed while still in the body bag to record evidence that might otherwise be lost or contaminated when the bag was opened. Afterward, the bag was unzipped and the victim's clothing carefully removed and searched for bullets, metal fragments, or other items of interest to the trooper investigators, who were awaiting the examiner's report.

When the clothing was hung up to dry, Dr. Norman Thompson, the forensic pathologist who conducted the initial exam and would do the autopsy, noted that the red shirt had a large bloodstain on the back. And though the second bullet hit the man in the stomach, there was very little blood on the front of his tee-shirt or the outer clothing. The bloodstains indicated the man had been shot first in the back. After the impact he spun around and fell backward, never rolling onto his stomach, then shot twice more. Virtually all the bleeding occurred while he was lying on his back.

When Thompson put his tools aside for sterilization and began the cleanup ending the initial examination, an aide wheeled the gurney into a walk-in refrigerator to await an autopsy the next day.

CHAPTER 3
The Investigation

On Friday morning, State Trooper Mike Sears drove from Anchorage to Hope, stopping at the Girdwood 7-11 and a highway construction site on the Seward Highway. He showed Kent Leppink's photo to store clerks, road flaggers, and equipment operators. All looked at the bearded man in the picture and shook their heads. Sears struck out everywhere until he headed down the Hope Cutoff and went three miles past the murder scene into the town of Hope.

The Discovery Cafe, one of the village's two restaurants, would be mobbed when tourist season started in a few weeks, but was virtually empty in early May. Sears showed the victim's photo to the cook, Maria Motoyama, who recalled seeing the man a week or so before. He came in looking for his girlfriend. The victim had shown Maria a picture of himself with a blond woman, asking if she had seen his fiancée. The cook hadn't, but they chatted for ten minutes anyway, passing the time.

The man said his fiancée was in the area helping friends fix a cabin roof. Sears asked Maria if she knew of any cabin roof work going on, but she did not. He also talked to the diner's only customer, with no luck. After the bearded man put the photo in his pocket and walked out, Maria and the customer joked about guys having girlfriend problems.

While Sears was in Hope, DeHart called Trooper Dallas Massie, a detective in the Palmer Detachment, and asked him to check out a house in a residential subdivision on the main road between Palmer and Wasilla, the house listed on the victim's checks. He was to look for a Mechele Hughes and a John Carlin, the owner of the house in Anchorage, the one Kent's driver's license showed as his address.

Massie and Trooper Mike Brandenburger found Mechele, the owner of the house, with Carlin, a balding man in his 30s, and Carlin's son, 17-year-old John Carlin IV. The house was being remodeled, and the three were working in a storage shed in the rear, gathering items to take back to Carlin's home in South Anchorage. They said they were looking for their own possessions, which they believed to be hidden there by their housemate, Kent Leppink. They said Kent lived with them when he wasn't sleeping on his boat or fishing in Prince William Sound. He sometimes stole things, they said, and they were trying to get some of them back.

Massie took the woman into the house for an interview while Brandenburger talked to Carlin and his son in the shed. Mechele asked Massie why they were asking questions about Kent and volunteered that she had just returned from a brief vacation at Lake Tahoe with her boyfriend, Scott Hilke.

The woman became increasingly anxious as the questioning continued. "Is Kent in any trouble?" she asked. "Has he done something? Why are you guys here?"

Massie told her that Kent had been found dead under suspicious circumstances. The woman seemed shocked and became upset. Her blue eyes flowed tears and she appeared confused.

When she calmed down, Massie asked, "Did he have any enemies?"

None that she knew of, she replied.

"Well, tell me what you do know," the trooper said. "Anything you can."

She said she couldn't think of any outright enemies, but Kent might have enraged somebody because "he's very sneaky and he lies a lot, and he keeps people's Social Security numbers, for what I don't know."

Massie had done a lot of death notifications, but there was something odd about this one. The woman had cried, but the depth of her sorrow at news of her housemate's death seemed unconvincing. He thought her tears lacked sincerity.

When the interviews were completed, Massie cautioned the three to leave Kent's belongings as they were. Detectives would want to look them over, he said, and they should be undisturbed. He said other investigators would want to talk to the three further when they got back to Carlin's house in Anchorage.

That evening Scott Hilke called from California, checking to see that Mechele arrived safely after her visit with him. Young John Carlin answered and, before calling Mechele to the phone, told Hilke that Kent was dead; he had been shot and killed.

When word got out in Anchorage that Kent Leppink had been murdered, his friends were astounded. "Only a loony would shoot this guy," said Buzz Williams of Chugiak, a commercial fisherman who first brought Kent to Alaska. "You would have to shoot him between the eyes because he was just as likely to take the gun away from you. He was as strong as a horse and as big as a door. He was about six foot five and could reach up and touch our nine-foot ceilings. But he had a mild manner and not a mean streak in his body."

CHAPTER 4
The Dancer from New Orleans

Mechele Hughes was a dancehall girl, a young New Orleans woman who went north to mine for gold in a frontier saloon and build a better life. Of medium height and strikingly attractive, with a sweet voice and air of innocence, she came to Alaska in 1994 to raise college money by mining the pockets of lonely men. Unlike the painted ladies who trailed the Gold Rush miners, Mechele was a stripper who wriggled and writhed to the raucous music of rock bands. Her targets—known in the trade as "marks"—were randy fishermen, oil workers and businessmen. She wanted a stake to pay for an education because that was the key to getting a respectable job, marrying a good man and living out her life as a suburban wife and mother in the Lower 48. Like many frontier women, she was a risk-taker.

Mechele worked at one of Alaska's most notorious nightclubs, The Great Alaska Bush Company. She wasn't much of a dancer, but she strode enticingly around the stage, looked great naked, and was a spellbinding conversationalist who could keep men talking and spending thousands of dollars to buy her time and attention. Mechele's personal mission and flirtation with danger put her in the midst of an explosive mix of personalities.

16 Dead Man's Dancer

The Bush Company is one of Alaska's renowned bars; many of its customers are men far from home and the arms of their wives and lovers. Its name is a double-entendre referring both to the Alaskan back country, known as The Bush, and to the female feature by the same name.

Mechele was born in New Orleans. Her father was the first of her mother Sandy McWilliams' two husbands; both marriages ended in divorce. Because Mechele's father was in the Air Force, the family moved from city to city. When Mechele was 12, her father died and Sandy married an airline employee, so frequent moves continued even after the first divorce. The year of her father's death Mechele developed scoliosis, a curvature of the spine that required frequent hospitalization; she spent a year and nine months in a body brace. Doctors implanted a steel rod in her back, leaving a scar running the length of her back and giving her an artificially induced perfect posture.

When the second marriage broke up, Sandy and Mechele moved back to New Orleans, where they had relatives and a long family history.

Mechele was a bright and active child who did well in school. Her grades were generally A's and B's, though she got C's in conduct because—her mother says—she talked too much.

Police say Mechele ran away from her New Orleans home at 14, stealing her sister Melissa's identification card—which showed her as four years older—and moved to New York to try a career in modeling. But Mechele says police are wrong and that she left home at age 16—with her mother's consent. That version is backed up by her mother, who told a newspaper reporter that she didn't approve of Mechele's leaving but knew she couldn't stop the headstrong young woman. Better to let her go and stay in touch.

Mechele got some work as a model, though fashion jobs

were scarce. When she could get runway assignments her face, form, and personality made her a standout, but there weren't enough such opportunities to make a living. She had bigger plans, much bigger plans, and her budding body and charm were her ticket to achievement.

Pat Giganti, a New Jersey construction company owner, was then living in New York and met Mechele at the Iguana Club on Park Avenue around 1990. He was then in his late 30s, she in her late teens. "I'm from New York City," Giganti told Megan Holland, a reporter for the Anchorage (AK) Daily News. "I come from a pretty fast place. And let me tell you, she made me feel like I was standing still."

Giganti and Mechele dated for about three years, living together and working together at a deli he owned in Bricktown, New Jersey. Giganti told Holland he thought Mechele had a split personality. He said she was a lot of fun to be with and could charm people, but "she's like a thoroughbred racehorse bred for being cruel."

Mechele left New Jersey in 1993, returning to New Orleans, where she worked in restaurants while she studied for the tests that would win her the equivalent of a high school diploma. Giganti said Mechele left New Jersey in a Volvo sedan she bought by signing his name, leaving him to make the payments. Her friends deny the accusation and say Giganti is still bitter about the breakup.

Mechele loved birds and animals, and wanted to become a veterinarian. But that would require an education, and studying veterinary science would cost money. She told her family she was going to take a job stripping at a New Orleans club, where she could earn more than in a restaurant. Her mother, sister, and grandmother were all unhappy about the decision, but Mechele was Mechele and they couldn't talk her out of it.

When Mechele turned 21 in 1994, a year after her return

to New Orleans, she decided she could make even more money dancing in Alaska, where the oil fields were fueling an economic boom, than she could in New Orleans—and she needed a bigger bankroll to speed things up. Mechele had plans for a better life than the strip clubs could offer; in the meantime, she would live life on the edge for a while. She and a dancer friend from the New Orleans club drove the Volvo to Anchorage and got jobs at the Great Alaskan Bush Company. Mechele adopted the stage name Bobby Joe. By that time she had learned the tricks of the dancing trade, including how to charm men into giving her furs, jewelry and cash, skills she used well at "The Bush," as most Alaskans call it.

During Alaska's Gold Rush era, dancehall girls and prostitutes were often members of a frontier town's aristocracy. That changed as the population grew and respectability gained favor, but even in the 1990s when the blond-haired Mechele swept into a restaurant with her retinue, she had the appearance and bearing of a young Alaskan royal. Mechele had a pleasant personality and seemed easy to deal with—but she was definitely the person in charge. And, there was something about her. She wasn't well known outside the raucous venue of The Bush Company, but the service staffs at the city's restaurants saw her often. They were inevitably glad to see a party with Mechele at its center. Accompanying the young beauty would be several of her female friends and a coterie of young men, at least a few of them her fiancées. The men were eager to please and impress the lady they loved, so they were good tippers.

Mechele danced on the club stage and often did up-close-and-personal lap dances for customers, but much of her work time was spent socializing with the men drawn to her. She had a mesmerizing effect on them and received large tips, a dancer's primary source of income. She stuffed her tips into one of the cloth bags sold with bottles of Crown Royal whisky.

When she went home from work each night, she would shake bills out of the bag onto the kitchen table and count them up, the total often running from $1,000 to $3,000.

The club's music wasn't well suited for dancing—more just to provide rhythm for women to use as sound effects while they wiggled and shook their bodies. Personal magnetism in lieu of dancing skills made Mechele one of the club's leading attractions. Men paid hundreds of dollars to spend time with her, listen to her voice, and become convinced that they were special and worth the attention of a good-looking woman.

Her most ardent suitors were granted relationships extending outside work hours. With John Carlin, Kent Leppink, traveling salesman Scott Hilke, North Slope worker Brett Reddell, and a few others who were never named (one who went by the sobriquet "Elvis"), she had enough men eager to support her that Mechele eventually found she could retire from stripping. She quit the Bush Company in January of 1996 and enrolled in courses at the University of Alaska Anchorage, a big step in the next phase of her life's plan.

CHAPTER 5
The Traveling Salesman

Scott Hilke first came to Alaska in August 1994 to train Anchorage workmen in operation and repair of large-scale power plants. He was an expert in the field and worked for Conval, manufacturers of valves for power plants, refineries, and petrochemical plants. The George M. Sullivan power facility on the east side of the city was about to undergo major maintenance. Hilke was then getting a divorce from his wife in California and, like many unattached men visiting the city he spent an evening enjoying the fleshy delights of The Bush Company. There he met Mechele—and became one of her outside-work friends.

Hilke left soon after his arrival when the Sullivan plant maintenance work was postponed. He told Mechele he would be back in a few weeks. She gave him her telephone number and invited him to call when he returned.

He called as promised, and the two began an extended relationship. When he was in Alaska, Scott and Mechele saw each other often; the relationship becoming closer as time passed. He spent $3,000 on an engagement ring and gave it to her on Thanksgiving. They made plans to marry a year later, on Thanksgiving Day, 1995. The two had matching tattoos, a small purple dinosaur on their ankles. Scott got his tattoo early in their relationship, after he became acquainted with Mechele's.

Among their shared dreams was to build and own a bird sanctuary in Costa Rica, a sanctuary where Mechele could indulge her love for birds. Mechele carried the dream to some length, researching the cost of such a facility and the practicality of moving to and living in Costa Rica.

In March, Hilke had a falling out with the president of his company, quit his job, began living on savings from a 401(k) retirement account, and moved into the house Mechele had recently acquired in Wasilla. By that time, Mechele had another semi-permanent guest. Kent Leppink sometimes lived on his commercial fishing boat and other times appeared to be couch-surfing at Mechele's place. Kent was obviously infatuated with Mechele, and his presence made Hilke nervous. But Mechele did not seem romantically attached to Kent, so Hilke shrugged and accepted the odd living arrangement.

One day Hilke was working around the house to keep himself occupied. When attaching a piece of molding, he drove in a nail and was amazed to see it fly unhindered through the wall. Something was wrong with Mechele's new house. Scott went into the crawlspace, pulled back insulation and found heavy dry-rot infection. He was amazed the place was still standing.

Mechele hired a building inspector, who told her the house was indeed unsuitable for habitation and needed major remodeling. She mentioned the problem to Carlin when she saw him at The Bush Company. Carlin had given her money for the down payment on the house and jumped at the chance to have her even closer. He invited all three of them—Mechele, Hilke, and Kent—to live at his place in South Anchorage while the work was being done in Wasilla. Carlin was lonely, strongly attracted to Mechele, and longed for the company of other adults in his large house. Mechele and Hilke moved in, though Hilke soon went back to work and resumed his frequent travels. Kent stayed at the Wasilla house for a time until construction operations forced him out, then he moved with the others into Carlin's house.

Kent's constant presence and the attention he lavished on Mechele annoyed Hilke, but that problem was resolved when Hilke's former supervisor at Conval offered him a job at a company he had moved to, Copes Vulcan, which sold a different product in the same field. Scott joined his old boss and began traveling once again, staying with Mechele when he was in Alaska.

Hilke's relationship with Mechele went through several phases. Despite the engagement and setting of a wedding date, Thanksgiving of 1995 came and went with no wedding. But Scott continued to see her when the two of them could get together. He was clearly her favorite, and she often flew to meet him at locations along his sales route, with tickets bought using his large backlog of frequent-flyer miles. They generally stayed at resorts for a few days' tryst before parting and flying home.

His frequent travels were a problem for the romance, so the wedding, he said, "just never came to be." Hilke moved back to California in January, 1996, though he and Mechele remained in touch.

CHAPTER 6
The New Jersey Steelworker

John T. Carlin III was a blue-collar worker who came into a small fortune while still in his 30s. The money settled a lawsuit resulting from his years of painting the Benjamin Franklin Bridge, a suspension structure over the Delaware River between Philadelphia and Camden, New Jersey. The contractor gave the workers buckets of lead-based paint and assigned them to paint from one end of the bridge to the other, then turn around and paint their way back—from New Jersey to Pennsylvania—then back again, for years at a time.

Whether Carlin actually had lead poisoning is an open question. Ingested lead can affect many parts of the body, including the brain, sexual functions, and much more, and the results are not always predictable. When Carlin's lawyers settled the case they sent him a check for $1.2 million.

John had always wanted to see Alaska and decided his newfound wealth should take him there. He bundled his ailing wife Nancy and teenage son, John Carlin IV, into a car and headed for Anchorage in late 1994. The younger Carlin told friends the trip was supposed to be a two-week vacation, but his mother liked the doctor she saw while in Anchorage, and the family decided to stay for a while.

By some accounts the trip's motivation was to let Nancy

see the Northern Lights before she died, but one of Carlin's friends says it was John who wanted to come north, and the trip probably shortened Nancy's life. She died a few weeks after they arrived in Alaska.

The young widower bought a house on Brook Hill Court in a South Anchorage subdivision and started building a new life for himself in a city as far from the Ben Franklin Bridge as he could get. He missed his wife and their sex life, but he didn't make friends easily. One of the few men he met and trusted was Kirk Wickersham, a lawyer and real estate expert who was going through a divorce and was himself rather lonely. The two met when Carlin called the lawyer for help in buying his house.

Wickersham told Carlin he probably didn't need a lawyer for that. He said his own years of experience in law and real estate legal matters led him to conclude that many of the professional services performed in house sales were repetitive and—if the seller had sufficient guidance—could be handled largely without expensive representation by either a lawyer or a realtor. Wickersham was then developing a marketing and home sales program called "For Sale by Owner." He explained the program to Carlin and said that in most cases it wasn't necessary to pay much in the way of realtor commissions or legal fees to buy a house.

Carlin was intrigued by the idea and decided Wickersham's new business would be a good place to invest some of his newfound wealth. The two men hit it off despite the disparity in their backgrounds, and Wickersham accepted the $200,000 Carlin offered him to help get started in the new venture.

The two met often to talk about For Sale by Owner. Once, following a session in his office, when Carlin mentioned how much he missed his wife, Wickersham took him to The Bush Company. There Carlin met and was instantly drawn to the

Dead Man's Dancer

club's leading attraction, Bobby Joe, the dancer from New Orleans. When he first saw her in a revealing costume parading down the stairs from the floor above, Carlin's heart was hers.

His previous bridge-painting job had paid a good wage, but Carlin was unaccustomed to real wealth and did not handle it wisely. His growing enchantment with the dancer drew him back to The Bush Company whenever she was onstage, and he began spending virtually all his waking hours there, going through large sums of money on her and the club's other strippers. Like many lonely men at the bar, he would sit near the stage and place money at its edge for those who especially interested him. Some would perform a lap dance, a semi-private performance given in a quiet corner of the club and focused temptingly on the wide-eyed male who paid for it.

To make sure no opportunities are lost, women who are not then on the dancing stage watch as their colleagues perform, spotting which men place money down for the dancer. After the star performer of the moment chooses the customer she will concentrate on, the others approach and offer lap dances to each of the rest.

House rules forbade the customers from touching the girls, but the rules for what the dancers could and could not do were somewhat less restrictive. Such dances were an arousing entertainment that left the one-man audience panting.

Carlin was not a handsome guy. He looked like a pudgy, balding accountant but had the physique and brash demeanor of a man who worked on high steel. To maintain the women's interest in him during his almost daily visits to The Bush Company, Carlin would sometimes give them his ATM card and PIN number, and then ask them to get him some money from the club's cash machine. If his looks didn't impress the girls, perhaps his bank balance would.

Carlin was such an enthusiastic customer and a consistent

spender that Mechele told him her real name and began to see him outside working hours. He bought her expensive gifts including furs and jewelry, and gave her the down payment on the house in Wasilla.

Carlin had a volatile personality and could seem to be in a towering rage one minute, then back to normal soon afterward. One night he and Wickersham had dinner at Sorrento's Restaurant in Anchorage's Midtown district. Carlin parked his car in a spot clearly marked as a tow-away zone. When they returned, a tow-truck driver had hooked up the car and was about to drag it off. Carlin flew into a rage, grabbed a tire iron from his trunk and held it menacingly near the tow driver's head until the man unhooked his vehicle and left.

The display of rage shocked the genteel Wickersham, who fled into the restaurant and thought seriously about calling for help, though Carlin at that point seemed to be making his point with menace and did not seem ready to strike the tow driver. A few minutes later, after avoiding a seventy-five-dollar towing fee by threatening violence, Carlin's disposition returned to normal, and he was chatting pleasantly on the drive home, a personality change that amazed Wickersham.

His volatility also showed in telephone conversations with his lawyer in New York. He was convinced he should be receiving punitive damages from the bridge contractor as well as the compensatory damage settlement won earlier, which was to cover medical costs and lost wages. From Anchorage he would scream into the phone, trying to use the power of an angry voice to make things happen on the other side of the continent.

Carlin urged Wickersham to accept the $200,000 as an investment. But after Wickersham saw his would-be partner in a rage, the lawyer decided having such a volatile man in the real estate firm might be a bad idea. Wickersham told Carlin he

Dead Man's Dancer 27

would consider the money a loan and repay it as soon as For Sale by Owner's finances allowed, which he did.

Carlin tried working as a realtor in Wickersham's office, but he didn't take the real estate license test and couldn't legally remain on the job. Still, he was nominally employed there long enough to wreak havoc with For Sale by Owner's new health insurance policy.

The policy covered pre-existing conditions and Carlin's son, John Carlin IV, had been having emotional problems since the death of his mother. A family friend described the boy as confused and upset about the turns his life and his family's had taken since they left New Jersey. Young John wasn't happy about the decision to stay in Alaska and—devastated by his mother's death—dropped out of school. That worried Mechele, and she was troubled even more when the boy threatened suicide, twice that she knew of. He terrified his girlfriend, Adella Perez, as well by taking a large pistol from a closet, waving it around and pointing it at his own head, telling the girl how easy it would be to pull the trigger. Young John also used drugs (marijuana and LSD), punched a hole in a wall, smashed his hand against his car, and was involved in a car wreck.

Young John's worsening behavior prompted Mechele to insist that the boy be treated for mental illness, so Carlin took him to North Star Hospital, where he spent several weeks. The results of the treatment are unknown, but the cost of his commitment prompted the insurance company to cancel the relatively new policy. That sent Wickersham scrambling to find new coverage for his employees.

Wickersham was also drawn rather unwillingly into Carlin's social life. Because of the lawyer's own ongoing divorce, Mechele saw him as an affluent man at loose ends, a possible date for some of her friends. She would often call from a local pancake house in the middle of the night and urge the lawyer to come join her and Carlin, and meet one of her friends. Wickersham had mixed emotions but was grateful for the distraction and would doff his pajamas, get dressed, and trudge over to the pancake house, wondering what he had gotten himself into.

Though Carlin's sexual attraction to Mechele seemed genuine, he also had at least one affair with a male prostitute and frequented an online site called Gaymall. How Mechele learned about the male affair is unknown, but she may have seen evidence while checking Carlin's computer activity. John became angry when Scott Hilke sent him an instant message saying Mechele had told him about the fling with a male prostitute.

Carlin invited Mechele to take a weeks-long trip to Amsterdam and other cities with him in August of 1995. He told her he bought the tickets planning to take his late wife and didn't want to waste them. During the trip, they had sex at least once, even though Mechele was still engaged to Scott Hilke and—Carlin would later learn—to Kent Leppink as well.

When Christmas of 1995 arrived, Mechele and Carlin called young John into Carlin senior's bedroom and told him they were getting married. Shortly afterward, Carlin gave Mechele a $3,200 fur coat and an $11,000 diamond ring. That was the third engagement ring Mechele had accepted without ever breaking off a single relationship with her other fiancés. Hilke had given up hope of marrying Mechele, but Kent still considered her his bride-to-be, a bond she continued to encourage with notes about buying a wedding dress.

CHAPTER 7
The Tennessee Taxidermist

Kent Leppink was a complicated man. Prematurely balding like Carlin, he looked older than his age—34 in 1994. His family owned a successful Midwestern grocery chain headquartered in Michigan and he, like two of his three brothers, started out in the business. But Kent was fired after embezzling $100,000 and an attempted arson. Without a job, he decided to pursue one of his favorite recreational activities; he was an outdoorsman and went to Tennessee to study taxidermy at a game farm near Nashville. While there, he attended a Safari Club International convention in Nevada, a popular gathering of big-game hunters, who frequently needed mounted trophies.

There he met Russ Williams, an Alaska fisherman who invited Kent to come north and work the summer of 1993 as crewman on his fishing tender boat. Williams' tender was a seagoing vessel used to ferry fish catches from netting boats to canneries. Its job was to pick up salmon from vessels that hauled in fresh, bright fish by the ton from the ice-blue waters of Prince William Sound. The catcher boats would unload their fish into tenders, which then rushed them to canneries in the nearest port, leaving the net boats to continue fishing. Kent jumped at the chance and moved to Anchorage as the season approached. Williams gave Kent the lasting nickname "TT," which stood for "Tennessee Taxidermist."

Kent's newfound enthusiasm for the fishing industry in rugged outdoor Alaska impressed his father, who felt bad about kicking him out of the family grocery business. After Kent's first season in fishing proved successful, his father Ken took his wife Betsy and son Ransom to visit Kent the following summer, when Kent was once again working on the tender.

Ransom and the Leppinks' other two sons were still edgy about Kent's thievery from the family business, so the parents decided to take each son, one by one, to see Kent and how well he was doing in Alaska. Ransom would be the first, though he proved to be the only brother to make the trip.

After visiting Kent aboard the tender in Whittier harbor, the father agreed to finance his son in his own commercial fishing venture. With dad's money behind him, Kent purchased a tender, formed a business and—for the first time in his life—began working for himself. He also stopped in at The Bush Company one night, met the dancer called Bobby Joe, and was enchanted. Within months his initial enchantment developed into full-blown obsession.

Despite his passionate love for Mechele, Kent's sexuality is a question. Depending on which of his friends and relatives you believe, Kent was either an avid heterosexual or a bisexual—or perhaps even gay. There is evidence to support all three arguments, which suggests that he enjoyed sex but wasn't always fussy about whether the object of his affections was a man or a woman. Whatever his true sexual orientation, Kent still became a willing participant in Mechele's manipulative schemes. The odd thing about his love life is that Kent never had sex with the woman he adored and wanted to marry, even though she was anything but virginal. She, however, had sex with a number of men who didn't hesitate to kiss and tell.

In the weeks before his death, Kent made what were

perceived as homosexual advances on young John Carlin, feigning sex with lurid hip movements near the already troubled teenager. The moves unnerved the boy and infuriated his father, who called police. Officers interviewed the boy but didn't pursue the case. The incident was seemingly resolved when the elder Carlin had a discussion with Kent about his crude sense of humor.

CHAPTER 8
The Barrow Boyfriend

Brett Reddell was another of Mechele's suitors. He lived and worked in Barrow on Alaska's remote north coast. When first contacted by detectives in 1996, a few months after the murder, Reddell said Mechele was his girlfriend, and he had expected her to move to Barrow to live with him.

Reddell gave Mechele the keys to his red pickup, inviting her to use it whenever she wished. When she needed money, as she often did, Mechele would call him in Barrow, and he would send it. As she did with the other men in her life, Mechele used Reddell as an ATM machine, a money dispenser who would give her cash when she wanted something.

Like many residents of Alaska's Bush country, the vast area unreachable by road, he kept a vehicle in Anchorage for use when he came to town and wanted to get around on the road system or drive down the Alaska Highway to points south of the Canadian border.

Reddell was project superintendent for an Alaska Native corporation that held contracts for oil company work on the North Slope. From his headquarters in Barrow, he ran all of the company's operations and occasionally flew to Anchorage to visit its main offices and enjoy some time off. During one of his trips he met Mechele at the Bush Company and, like the others, fell in love. The two began dating and she told him she would move north with him. She explained Hilke's frequent visits to her house by telling Reddell that Scott was dating a woman she was rooming with— though she had no female roommate.

Reddell told detectives during an interview in September, five months after Kent Leppink's death, that he expected Mechele to quit the Bush Company, buy him a house trailer in Arizona and move it to Talkeetna, north of Anchorage, where they would live together. Reddell said he was still supporting her after she quit working and started college, in the months before the shooting. He gave her his bank debit card and the PIN number, so she had constant access to his bank account. Mechele occasionally did visit Reddell in Barrow but had sex with him only once.

Her visits to Barrow were frequent enough that they became part of Mechele's scheme to avoid having Kent discover when and where she was actually traveling. When she was gone, Kent checked the airport parking lot frequently. In the days before he was shot, while she was visiting Hilke at Lake Tahoe, Mechele and Carlin wrote the note suggesting that she was staying at Carlin's fictional cabin near Hope.

She told Carlin—if Kent found her car at the airport—he was to tell the fisherman that she was in Barrow. That would have undermined the ruse that she was at a cabin in Hope. It might also have served to wave off Carlin and relieve them both of the burden of the murder plot. Telling Kent that she was in Barrow would have eliminated any reason he had to look for her in Hope and removing the temptation of drawing Kent to the remote location.

After Kent's murder, Reddell told a co-worker at Prudhoe Bay that his girlfriend had been using his truck while it was parked in Anchorage and—because he left the keys with her—the truck somehow wound up in New Orleans when the girlfriend moved back there. The friend said Reddell was amazed by the move, and the disappearance of his truck, and wanted the vehicle back, if nothing else. But before he could retrieve it from New Orleans, Reddell learned that Carlin had taken the missing truck to New Jersey. He said he called Carlin, who told him the truck was there and Reddell should come and get it or make arrangements for someone to pick it up. Reddell's co-worker had a friend who was visiting near Carlin's New Jersey home; the friend agreed to retrieve it and sell the truck for him.

Reddell had his own legal problems, which undermined the value of his testimony when the case went to court. Detectives asked him to help in their investigation by talking to Mechele and feeding back what she told him (though apparently not wearing a wire). But Reddell was in prison for child molestation at the time of the police interview, which made his testimony in an unrelated case almost worthless. He might also have seemed motivated by a $10,000 reward offered by the Leppink family for the arrest of their son's murderer.

CHAPTER 9
An Engaging Woman

Kent decided that Mechele was the woman of his dreams and proposed to her in November of 1994, a month after they met. He gave her a pendant and a diamond ring. She accepted his proposal, so he notified his family and began making marriage plans. He told her they should celebrate their love by postponing sex. No firm date was set for the wedding so the engagement at that point was open-ended. (A week after accepting Kent's proposal, Mechele accepted Scott Hilke's engagement ring as well.)

Mechele seemed to be a young man's dream, a beautiful, sexy woman, unfazed by nudity, one who could carry on an intelligent conversation for hours. Where most men must leave their hopes and desires at the door of The Bush Company when they leave, Mechele came into their lives, moving into Carlin's home without hesitation when she needed shelter.

The presence in the same household of the four men and one provocative woman proved to be a toxic emotional brew. Antipathy toward Kent by the others was growing and had reached fever pitch by April, 1996. Each of the housemates had his or her own reasons and—as John Carlin IV said of Kent—nobody liked him, not even the woman who was pressing him for wedding gown money.

He spied on everyone except young John, though that can't

be ruled out. While in the Wasilla house in 1995, Kent found a way to watch covertly as Mechele and Hilke had sex. Later, in Carlin's house, he rummaged through their email, personal papers, credit card bills and anything else they received in the U.S. mails.

Hilke suspected that Kent stole a small pistol from Mechele's car, a weapon Hilke gave her for personal protection. Kent was bothered by his housemate's suspicions and tried to phone Hilke's parents about the missing handgun, perhaps trying to enlist their help in convincing their son he didn't do it.

When Hilke was traveling, about every five or six weeks he and Mechele would arrange to meet for a few days together at a vacation resort somewhere away from the bizarre domestic situation in Alaska. Her absences aggravated Kent's obsession with her, and his spying became more intense.

His household espionage became as obsessive as his love for her. On one occasion, when Mechele and Scott were trysting at a resort in Metairie, Louisiana, Kent flew down, arrived when they were still asleep and served them a surprise breakfast in bed. The incident seemed not a benign and friendly gesture but a stalker's way of saying "gotcha."

The two lovers were unhappy about the unexpected intrusion on their time alone, but decided to take advantage of Kent's presence. Mechele had driven her Volvo to Metairie, so she asked Kent to drive it back to Alaska while she rode back with Scott. He did so and stopped to visit his family in Michigan along the way. Mechele and Hilke took a different route across country to the Alaska Highway and home to Anchorage, one they did not disclose to Kent. She used an assumed name at overnight stops to avoid his tracking system.

As Hilke's business travel schedule and long absences picked up in the fall of 1995, Mechele began spending more time with Carlin, culminating in their trip to Europe. She managed to

Dead Man's Dancer

deflect some of Kent's concern about the European adventure by telling him it was just a trip with a friend, but Hilke's worries were another matter. Hilke said after the trip that when Mechele announced she was going to Europe with the balding steelworker he "was not enthused." Hilke's discomfiture did not deter Mechele, who had an iron will beneath her soft surface. "Don't worry about John," she lied, "he's impotent."

When Mechele left with Carlin, she asked Hilke to care for the house while she was gone. His duties included caring for her pets—a growing collection of dogs and birds. Meanwhile, Kent was spending many nights sleeping on his boat and, though he had a bedroom for his use when he was in town, he would often sleep on Carlin's living room couch, a better place to keep track of the household.

CHAPTER 10
The Last Month

On February 14, 1996, Mechele and Kent met with Anchorage life insurance agent Steven Leirer and asked about buying policies of $1 million on each of them. They told Leirer they were going into business together—Kent's fishing business—and were applying for a loan to buy a new boat. Leirer ordered medical exams for them both. He said his company, New York Life, could write a million-dollar policy on Kent's life, but the underwriters would not insure Mechele for that much. Her policy, perhaps because her role in the fishing company would be more peripheral and they were not yet married, would be only $150,000. Kent was annoyed—he wanted a million-dollar policy on each of them—but decided they would take what they could get.

He asked that Mechele be listed as eighty-percent beneficiary of the million-dollar policy, with the other twenty percent going to his parents. He was to be listed as beneficiary of the smaller policy on Mechele.

On April 18th Kent went with Mechele to Anchorage lawyer Brian Brundin's office. Kent wanted to rewrite his will—which listed members of his family as beneficiaries—and leave all of his property to Mechele. Brundin thought Kent was making some kind of statement by designating her

Dead Man's Dancer

as the sole beneficiary in his will. While there, the two got into an argument, and she said, "I can compete if it was a girl." Brundin suspected the argument indicated Kent was having a homosexual relationship—and Mechele was angry about it.

The next day, Kent returned alone to Brundin's office and grumbled that Mechele had been to North Star Hospital, where young John Carlin was being treated. While there she had asked if Kent also sought counseling from hospital staff. North Star told Mechele that Kent had inquired, but was referred to another facility. The fisherman wanted to know whether he could sue the hospital for telling her that much. Brundin said he probably could not.

The lawyer asked Kent what Mechele meant when she said she could compete if it was a girl, but Kent didn't respond. Instead he complained that Mechele was cheating on him with Scott Hilke and with the elder Carlin, and had stolen things from him, including a $4,000 statue, some antiques and a $6,700 laptop computer. Kent said she had also gone shopping at Eagle Hardware and purchased $4,600 worth of kitchen cabinets on his account without his knowledge, a purchase that infuriated him.

The lawyer said he had seen a lot of marriages come and go, and it didn't look like Kent was headed for a very happy one with this young woman. Brundin warned Kent that he didn't hold much hope she would change, even if changing would benefit her. The lawyer said Mechele was like the scorpion in an old fable. In it the scorpion and a turtle are on one bank of a river and both want to cross.[2]

"The scorpion says to the turtle, 'I can't swim. If you let me on your back and take me across this river, I'll appreciate it.' And the turtle looked at him and said, 'What, are you crazy?

---

[2] The following is a direct quote from the trial transcript and statement by lawyer Brian Brundin.

We get halfway across and you'll bite me and sting me, and we'll die and I will drown.'

"And the scorpion said, 'Why would I do that, for crying out loud?' and so he jumped on the back of the turtle and, halfway across, sure enough, he stung the turtle and they both drowned. The moral of the story is like a leopard not changing his spots. The scorpion is a scorpion, period, and he will bite you even if he says he won't."[3]

Kent left Brundin's office feeling glum and worried. Then whatever was making him nervous suddenly got much more worrisome. His detective work had turned up something that convinced him everything had changed, that his life was not what he thought it was, that things were happening behind his back.

Shortly thereafter Kent showed up at lawyer Kirk Wickersham's office and told him, "I'm going to get killed." Wickersham couldn't believe what he was hearing and urged Kent to get out of Carlin's house. If the threat was real, Kent could easily save himself by leaving, by getting away from the dangerous people he lived with. Wickersham also urged him to report any plot against him to the police, but Kent did neither one. Leaving the house was impossible at that point; Kent's obsession with Mechele wouldn't let him.

Kent also returned to the New York Life office and changed the beneficiary of his insurance policy from Mechele to his parents. He tucked the beneficiary change form into the pocket of his jeans and kept it for his father.

---

[3] A more accurate accounting of the fable is: A scorpion comes up to a turtle on the bank of a river. The scorpion asks the turtle, "Will you carry me across the river on your back?" to which the turtle replies, "Why would I do that? When we get half way across, you'll sting me, and I'll die!" The scorpion tells him, "If I did that, we would both drown." Finding this reasonable, the turtle allows the scorpion to climb onto his back, and they set off across the river. Halfway across, the scorpion stings the turtle. The turtle cries, "Why did you do that? Now we'll both drown!" The scorpion replies, "Sorry, it's just in my nature."

CHAPTER 11
Dad Leppink Visits

Kent's father, Ken Leppink, flew to Anchorage on April 26 to help his son get ready for fishing season and try to get a better understanding of the boy's romantic situation. Young Kent still considered Mechele the love of his life and was deeply immersed in plans for the big wedding.

When Ken and his wife met Mechele on an earlier visit to Alaska, they got the impression she wasn't as committed to the relationship as their son was. Now Kent seemed even more deeply wrapped in an unlikely romantic web. Though the parents were skeptical of Mechele's seriousness about marrying their son, Kent told Ken that Mechele would be flying back to Michigan with him to look at a church for the ceremony and a place to hold the reception in the family's hometown, Lakeview, near Grand Rapids.

Dad arrived in Anchorage on a Northwest Airlines flight from Minneapolis and was met at the airport by Kent and John Carlin. Carlin invited Mr. Leppink to stay at his house with Kent, young John and Mechele, but the older man declined saying he had a room reserved at the Golden Lion motel.

Mechele wasn't there for Ken's arrival, but Kent told his father that she was on a road trip and would be along in a day or two. He said he would be scraping and painting the boat that week, getting ready for the season ahead, and would not be coming with her to Michigan.

Dad Leppink came to Anchorage expecting to work on the boat, but his son was worried about his aging father and afraid he might be in the way or get injured in the bustle of scraping, cleaning, painting and rigging a boat in preparation for a summer on the water. Dad had years of business experience and knew his numbers, so Kent asked him to help do his income tax return instead.

Ken was shocked. "Kent, this is the 26th of April. Usually income tax is due on the 15th of April." He said he would handle the taxes but warned Kent there might be penalties because of the late filing.

They stopped at Carlin's house briefly, and then headed for the Golden Lion. As they arrived at the motel, Kent handed Ken an envelope.

"Here," he said, "this is for you."

His father opened the envelope and saw a change of beneficiary form for a million-dollar insurance policy. It named Ken and his wife as the beneficiaries. Kent said the insurance was a gift paid for by Mechele's grandfather.

"Kent, I don't like the smell of this," his father said. "This is not good."

"It's OK," his son replied. "It's all right."

The two men talked about the policy briefly, and then dropped the subject, leaving the older Leppink very uncomfortable about it. Ken didn't need money—his grocery chain had been a profitable business venture; he and his wife had a comfortable retirement—but he was worried about what the very existence of the million-dollar policy might mean. And why in the world would Mechele's grandfather want the Leppinks to be beneficiaries?

At the motel they sorted out the papers for Kent's tax return, and Ken worked on IRS forms and documentation all the next day and into the evening, then again on Sunday after church. On Monday they visited an Anchorage accountant who agreed to finish and file the return, and to ride herd on Kent's future paperwork to avoid such problems next time.

This would be the first season for Kent on the Togiak. Ken had loaned the boy $35,000 for the down payment on the boat and co-signed for a $100,000 note to complete the deal. The Togiak was a service boat with a large hold. Young Kent's prior experience was as a crewman, working for wages and a share of other boats' earnings. At age 36 he would be skipper of his own boat for the first time.

On Monday, Kent stayed with his father at the motel, and then took him to the airport for the return trip to Michigan on Tuesday. He was embarrassed that Mechele was still nowhere to be seen. During his father's visit, he returned occasionally to Carlin's house to send an email to Mechele and hope for a reply that might tell where she was. He was sure she was at a cabin in Hope and told his dad she had gone there with a girlfriend, but he had no address or instructions on how to find the place. All he knew, he told Ken, was that the cabin belonged to Carlin. Kent's father left Anchorage and flew home to Michigan, never having seen his son's bride-to-be on the trip he made to help her prepare for the wedding.

CHAPTER 12
The Letter

On Saturday May 4th, two days after Kent's body was found, Detective Sergeant Dehart got a call from Ken Leppink in Michigan. The young man's father and his horrified mother, Betsy, had just opened a package newly arrived in the mail from Kent. Inside were a letter of instructions and a sealed envelope.

The handwritten instructions said: "Please put the enclosed envelope in your safe deposit box. Do not open it. I talked to you about 'insurance policies.' This is mine. If I didn't think that things could get a little 'rough' up here, I wouldn't have sent you this. It'll be safer there.

"It's not funny to talk about getting killed, but in today's world you have to expect anything. . . . If you think anything fishy has happened to me, then you can open up the other envelope I've sent."

Ken and Betsy, in shock since they were notified of their son's death, fearfully opened the inner envelope. There they found an angry but coherent note saying,

"Since you're reading this, you assume that I'm dead .... It was my time, and there's nothing that can change that. There are a few things I'd like you to do for me, though. I hate to be vindictive in my death, but paybacks are hell. Use the information enclosed to take Mechele DOWN. Make sure she is prosecuted:

- Fraud—She took me for a lot of money on the impression we were getting married. This may be hard to prove without me present, but give it a shot. It is a Class B felony in Alaska. $15,000 can be proved because you sent it to us.

- Insurance fraud ... have the IRS audit her. Turn her in!"

Kent's note said Mechele had fraudulently used John Carlin's medical insurance and was probably not reporting her dancing income to the Internal Revenue Service. He listed Mechele's Social Security number and her mother's address for aid in an investigation. He accused Mechele, John Carlin and Scott Hilke of his murder.

"Make sure they get burned. Make sure Mechele goes to jail for a long time, but visit her there. Tell her how much I really did (do) love her. Tell her you love her, and help her."

He told his parents to give or sell his boat to one of his friends, to take some of his $1 million life insurance money to pay off his debts, and to use a portion for a nice beach vacation.

"Act like I'm still there with you," he wrote, "and do the things I would like to do."

The "letter from the grave," as the news media later came to call it, was almost too much to bear. The parents' worries came crashing down on them. The errant son, who had moved to the Last Frontier to make a new life, instead had met his death. He had been murdered. Kent was sure he knew who his killers would be, and the Leppinks vowed they would carry out his last wish.

The letter added to the growing frustration of Alaska police detectives, whose suspicions about the murder were unsupported by direct evidence. If there was no smoking gun—no gun at all—and no fingerprints, traces of DNA, no known eyewitnesses—no nothing—surely, there was someone who knew enough to help break the case. If there was such a person, the job would be to find him or her and see what they knew.

There was no indication as to what convinced Kent that he was about to be killed. In his incessant probing into the affairs of his housemates, he had obviously run across something that convinced him a murder plot was in the works—and he was to be the victim.

The pointing finger of the victim made the case a high priority for the Alaska State Troopers. This seemed such a cold-blooded and pre-planned crime, one so bold that the victim knew about it well ahead of time, that there would surely be a trail of evidence. An investigation is often a plodding affair, one piece of evidence leading to another. But police needed a key piece to cut through the mists, the undeniable proof that the killing occurred the way they could then only suspect it did—an eyewitness, the murder weapon with fingerprints on it, something tangible that would be convincing in court. The fact that there were at least three suspects, perhaps four did not provide the "probable cause" required by the Constitution before an arrest could be made. It narrowed the focus of the investigation, but it couldn't be used to prove which of the four—if any of them—killed Kent Leppink.

Letting Kent's killer or killers get away was out of the question, but for the moment the investigators were stymied. They were determined to work their way through the maze and bring the murderers to justice, even if it meant waiting.

CHAPTER 13
The Interviews

On May 5, DeHart and Belden went to Carlin's Anchorage home for interviews. They talked to John and tried to interview his son, but Carlin insisted on being present at the boy's interrogation, which was his right as a parent. The detectives hoped to talk to young John alone, but couldn't do so if the father insisted on being there. The older Carlin's presence would make the son reluctant to say anything his father might disapprove of, anything that might reflect badly on either of them. And, as the detectives expected, the interview yielded little of value.

The officers knew that Kent Leppink had purchased a Gateway laptop computer and asked Carlin where it was. At that point Mechele entered the room, and they asked her the same question. She said she and Kent co-owned the laptop, that it was having startup problems, and she sent if off to her sister Melissa Williams, a computer whiz living in Moab, Utah, who could fix it.

Mechele asked why the troopers wanted the computer and assured them there was nothing on it. She said the computer had already been sent off to Melissa. But when the officers later checked with Mailboxes, Etc., records there showed it was actually presented for shipment on May 6, the day after their interview with her.

DeHart and Belden asked to see Kent's possessions, so Carlin and Mechele agreed to meet them at the Wasilla house. Police and the two civilians drove separately and met at the subdivision. DeHart went with Carlin to the storage shed, asking questions as they walked, while Belden interviewed Mechele inside the house.

During the interview, Belden asked Mechele whether she knew of a .44 magnum handgun in the household. She said she did, and when Carlin returned to the house Mechele asked him, "Have you seen Kent's big black gun?" The Troopers reported Carlin appeared to be displeased that the subject of the pistol had come up. He hung his head and said he hadn't seen it.

A strip club sometimes fans the baser instincts of men who, when fueled with alcohol, could be a danger to performers leaving after work. So Mechele and several of her dancer friends had decided to take a course required for a license to carry a concealed weapon. She showed up for a gun-handling and shooting session with the big Desert Eagle. She told the instructor that Kent loaned it to her with a box of ammunition. The instructor laughed and said the gun was much too large for her; a small person would find it difficult to hold steady and its sharp recoil painful. The range officer loaned her a smaller handgun more suitable for a woman.

Many who learned of the range incident assumed that the gun was loaned to Mechele by Carlin. Though sometimes irrational, Carlin was very solicitous of Mechele. He was an ex-Marine and had been a rangemaster at a large professional shooting range in New Jersey. Whatever his other judgmental failures, Carlin would have known the gun was too big and its recoil could injure her when she fired it. It seems unlikely he would have loaned her the gun.

Kent on the other hand, did many strange things in his life, quite a few more than Carlin. He also had experience with

Dead Man's Dancer

firearms, but believing that he loaned Mechele a handgun too large and powerful for her requires less stretch of the imagination than for Carlin. Though Carlin was the presumed owner of the .44 automatic, Kent was known to carry it on his boat for at least one summer's fishing season.

In his initial discussions with detectives, Carlin denied ever owning a Desert Eagle .44. Later, Sergeant DeHart said, "Uh, John, what would you say if I told you that I've been told that you also had a .44 gun in your house?"

Carlin answered, "I would say that's a bunch of crap."

DeHart replied, "You say you deny having a .44-caliber handgun in your home?"

Carlin: "Absolutely."

DeHart: "Never owned one?"

Carlin: "Nope."

DeHart: "At any time?"

Carlin: "No, not here in Anchorage." Then, he added that he owned a .44 back in his rangemaster days in New Jersey; he thought it was a Smith & Wesson.

On May 6, a jewelry store called Carlin's house to say a chain and bracelet Mechele ordered on April 28 had arrived. Mechele went to the store and, while there, tried to use a $250 credit Kent had coming for a pair of opal and diamond earrings she returned earlier. Kent had given her the earrings, but she said she had an allergic reaction to the materials and returned them.

When Mechele came in to pick up the chain and bracelet, the jeweler said he'd heard about Kent's murder. "Yes, that was a very creepy thing," Mechele replied. The jeweler said she couldn't use the credit because it might be tied up in Kent's estate.

In early June, Carlin put up $18,000 for the down payment on a $72,000 recreational vehicle, a luxury camper by the standards of the day. Mechele was to be responsible for payments on the balance. Carlin also designated her as young John's official guardian and, one of his friends said, set up a $200,000 trust fund for her to use on his care and provide support until he came of age.

A few days later, she left Anchorage for California, taking young John Carlin with her. Mechele told the boy's father she intended to take him to New Orleans and put him in a Catholic school there. And she intended to make sure the boy stayed in school this time. She had harangued young John about his frequent truancy since she first moved into the Carlin household. At one point, when school officials notified Carlin that his son was seriously delinquent and staying away from classes for months at a time, Mechele removed the distributor cap from the boy's car, leaving it disabled in the Carlin garage until he returned to school. If verbal pressure wouldn't keep him in school, perhaps loss of his car privileges would do the job. The ploy worked, but only temporarily.

When Mechele left Alaska with him, young John was uneasy about Mechele's plan to put him in Catholic school, but he rode with her in the RV during the long drive down the Alaska Highway to the Lower 48. He stayed with her while she visited Scott Hilke in Sacramento then headed northeast to her sister Melissa's house in Utah, where Melissa, her husband and son ran a campground.

Mechele knew before she left Anchorage about the accusatory letter Kent had written to his parents. It was a cloud hanging over her future.

When the package containing the computer arrived at Melissa's house, Mechele telephoned asking her sister to wipe the computer's hard drive clean, to take everything off it. Mechele said the laptop was entirely hers now and she wanted to start her new life with a clean slate, with all the old messages removed. The request troubled Melissa, so she delayed removing any files from the computer.

When Mechele reached Moab in her RV and found Melissa had not attempted to erase the hard drive, she was furious. They were sitting at a picnic table in Melissa's yard. While they talked, the question of Kent's death came up. Melissa disclosed to investigators, "She told me that he got what he deserved, that people didn't like him, that he hunted and stuffed animals, and that he—she felt that he got exactly what he deserved."

Melissa said Mechele slammed her hands down on the picnic table and angrily stood up. "She said that it was too bad that someone didn't torture him first."

Mechele and young John spent several days at Moab. Scott Hilke showed up and took her river-rafting. Melissa told police that when Mechele was talking about the murder victim, young John added his opinion that nobody liked Kent. Mechele also mentioned to her sister that Kent had written a letter blaming her if anything happened to him.

Alaska State Troopers had been trying to reach Melissa. After Mechele left Moab, Melissa returned a call to one of the investigators. She asked if her sister might be involved in an Alaska murder case.

Young John wanted no part of Mechele's plan to put him into a Catholic school in New Orleans; his intention to avoid that fate grew stronger during the long road trip. Shortly after they arrived in Mississippi, he left to visit his family in New Jersey and never came back. His pretext for getting beyond Mechele's control was attending a family wedding, after which he moved into his grandparents' home. When the elder Carlin returned from Alaska shortly afterward, John moved into the family home with his father.

CHAPTER 14
After Alaska

Mechele had at least one supporter in the Leppink family, Kent's brother Lane, who warned Mechele that the family would try to blame her for Kent's murder. Lane was the black sheep of the family, often on the outs with the rest of the Leppinks. The others stopped giving him information about the case when they realized he was talking to Mechele.

Lane had been on the phone with her on May 4—the same day Sergeant DeHart called him—when his brother Ransom came by to talk about funeral arrangements. Lane broke off the telephone conversation, and then called Mechele back the next day. He told her what he had heard about the letter Kent wrote to his parents pointing at her as one of his murderers.

Lane and his wife came to Alaska about 11 months after Kent's death to do their own investigation, which was unfruitful.

Lane and Kent had not been getting along when Kent moved to Alaska. They argued over Kent's embezzlement from the family business, which Lane had discovered. Lane was estranged from the rest of the family because the Leppinks did not like his wife, Denise Garbo, owner of a hairstyle salon in one of the family stores. The Leppinks decided that her lease on the property would not be renewed, which infuriated both Lane and Denise.

DeHart had Hilke's phone number, so he called and asked for a meeting on July 29 at the Sacramento Police Department. Hilke showed up and gave the interview, but became irritated by the investigators' accusatory attitude. (He didn't know at that point that Kent had listed him as one of his possible murderers.) Hilke refused to give his home address to the officers, so DeHart asked Sacramento police to tail him and get one. Hilke spotted the tail and marched back to police headquarters, noticeably upset.

Realizing that the detectives would eventually get his address anyway, he told them where he lived and said they could come over on certain conditions, the main one being that they call first. Hilke spoke contemptuously of the people he knew in Alaska, calling them morons. Kent, he said, was an irritating guy.

DeHart and Belden called Hilke the next day and said they were coming over; they arrived about 40 minutes later. Hilke authorized them to look around the house and said he had talked to Mechele that morning, but he refused to say what they talked about. The detectives interviewed Hilke again, this time with his wife sitting protectively on the floor between his knees. Hilke and his wife in California were working on a divorce, though it never became final and they apparently reconciled.

After squandering his million-dollar fortune, much of it on Mechele's house, furs, jewelry, the recreational vehicle, travel and clothing, John Carlin was broke and needed to go back to work. The best-paying job he ever had was as a steelworker on the high bridges, so he sold his Anchorage house and made the long drive back to New Jersey, hoping to find a job comparable to the one he quit for his Alaska adventure.

Carlin had expected to be arrested for months, so he kept a list of people to be contacted in the event he was thrown in jail.

The list included names and phone numbers for his various lawyers and friends, as well as Mechele and his son John.

In New Orleans, Mechele enrolled at Loyola University, a Jesuit college, and began work toward a degree in veterinary medicine. She volunteered at a nearby zoo and worked several nights a week stripping in a local club. The large tips she could still command were enough to enable her to attend classes full-time during the day.

Mechele's love for animals never abated. She had five parrots, three dogs and a cat of her own and continually picked up stray dogs and tried to find their owners by printing posters and tacking them up around New Orleans.

At Loyola, she met Colin Linehan, a handsome medical student at the much larger and adjacent Tulane University. Colin wanted to be a family doctor and was a member of the Army Reserve Officer Training Corps; he would be obligated to serve a hitch in the military after completing his medical training. Mechele and Colin hit it off and moved in together, living in part on her earnings.

Colin was not a wealthy man with prospects for a prosperous practice; he was training to become a military physician. In school he was so broke he couldn't afford a car. They were married in the spring of 1998, with Mechele paying for her own engagement ring and the wedding itself. The following year they had a baby, a daughter.

After graduation, Colin went to Maryland for his medical residency. Mechele gave up her hope of becoming a veterinarian and went to Maryland with him. She kept up her studies and taught Sunday school at a local Catholic Church.

Colin was next assigned to Madigan Army Medical Center at Joint Base Lewis-McChord near Tacoma and was soon deployed to Iraq. Though many media outlets would portray

Dead Man's Dancer

Mechele as an affluent suburban doctor's wife, Colin was a dedicated military physician living on a young officer's salary. While Colin was deployed, Mechele reportedly had several affairs, including one with another doctor, a friend of the family, and she reconnected for a time with Scott Hilke. The affairs apparently occurred at a time when Mechele and Colin were having marital problems and nearly divorced, but the two reconciled when he returned from Iraq.

In Olympia, Mechele became a suburban housewife; one of her friends said she would bake cookies to welcome new families to her neighborhood. When the baby was young, she worked as a waitress at a steak house two nights a week, so Colin wouldn't have to work extra hours at the hospital to support the family and could spend time with his daughter.

Mechele earned her master's degree at Evergreen State College and became an intern at the Washington State Executive Ethics Board. She volunteered at her daughter's Catholic school and worked 12-hour shifts at a crisis center, counseling people impacted by suicide or suicide threats, and rape victims. She went to St. Michael's Catholic Church and asked to become involved in its social justice programs, telling church officials she wanted to learn how she could help make a better world.

Mechele also became an outdoor athlete in the Pacific Northwest tradition: kayaking, biking, hiking and rock-climbing. She filled her house with books, loved to garden, and threw parties in her backyard.

Once she complained to local police about a contractor stealing from her home, then told a prosecutor on the case that she forgave the thief. "She was very compassionate, very understanding, and very forgiving," the prosecutor reported.

While Mechele and her family were building a life in

suburbia, young John Carlin was growing into manhood and independence, eventually moving west to live with a girlfriend who was a student at Washington State University. John got a job as an electronic draftsman with a nearby engineering firm.

CHAPTER 15
The Cold Case Unit

The unsolved murder case was set aside and remained largely dormant for nine years, a nagging memory for the Alaska State Troopers who worked on it. They had tantalizing evidence—including the pointing finger of the long-dead victim—and several possible suspects, but still nothing sufficient to bring anyone to trial, nothing that would qualify as "direct" evidence. Then, in 2005, the file was assigned to the newly organized Cold Case Unit and a retired State Trooper detective and summertime fishing guide named Jim Stogsdill.

Stogsdill had the tall, lean look of a Western sheriff. People in Soldotna, Alaska, greeted him like a politician. A retired state trooper and former vice mayor of the city, he was also one of Alaska's top Kenai River guides. Stogsdill chased salmon when the river ran green with glacial melt in summer and pursued criminals when the water turned clear and cold, and the fish stopped running. Stogsdill studied old police files, followed leads and conducted interviews for the Cold Case Unit, a small team of top detectives who work on and try to solve crimes of years past.

Stogsdill and his colleagues had access to new science and techniques that were unavailable to those who tackled the original cases. If a crime isn't solved immediately, trails go cold, witnesses die or move away, people change, forget and take turns in their lives that are hard to follow. But, the difficult cases that wait in police files are not dead. Besides their technical advantages—and the newly developed resources they could now call on—the detectives of the Cold Case Unit were very good at what they did. They were also able to take advantage of the fact that sometimes witnesses get older and become more willing to talk than they once were.

The unit was formed in 2002 when the Alaska State Troopers received a federal grant dedicated to reopening and pursuing inactive police cases, especially unsolved cases that might yield to the investigative skills of experienced officers using new technology and techniques. The department elected to assign the work to experienced but now retired detectives, men and women with solid investigative skills willing to work part of the year on a contract team basis.

Stogsdill was one of the first officers recruited. He had become a law enforcement officer with the U.S. Air Force in 1968, and then spent 22 years with the Troopers, much of that time in the Homicide Unit of the Criminal Investigation Bureau, retiring in 1993. Like many retired police officers, he started a second career. His experience and seasonal occupation as a fishing guide made him a natural for the Cold Case Unit. He was a high-energy man with great skill and time on his hands when fishing ended for the year.

Stogsdill worked on the first case solved by the squad in 2002, one involving two 1985 shootings in Soldotna. The murderer had left a fingerprint in the cash drawer of the store when he cleaned out the register and shot the owner. The shopkeeper survived, and ten days later the same man broke into the home of a woman in another part of town. He killed her and stole about $400 from the woman's purse, leaving his prints on several of her papers.

Dead Man's Dancer 59

Later the murderer filed for a bus driver's license in Oklahoma and submitted to a required fingerprint test. When the prints were run against a national database in 2002, the computers said the man was the Soldotna murderer. Stogsdill arrested the suspect in a small Midwestern town and returned him to Alaska for trial.

In 2003 Stogsdill was assigned to the cold-trail Leppink case, which the department was determined not to forget. The "persons of interest" were long gone and unfruitful follow-ups had been attempted, to no avail. The most interesting of the bunch was young John Carlin IV, who had never been interviewed without having his father present.

One detective traveling on the East Coast on other business had stopped by the Carlin family home in New Jersey, but the boy's grandfather—John Carlin III's father—refused to allow the boy to be interviewed without the father present.

But, by the time Stogsdill got the case, John IV was 27 years old and living with a girlfriend in Tacoma. He was also estranged from his father. Stogsdill spent nearly a year studying the case files in his spare time and, when his field work got seriously under way, decided that talking to young John Carlin should be a priority.

"The kid was a loose end," Stogsdill said in a 2009 interview conducted in a Soldotna cafeteria. "Nobody had talked to him."

Anchorage Detective Linda Branchflower was a retired investigator for the Anchorage Police Department when she signed on for contract work with the Troopers' Cold Case Unit. Branchflower traced young Carlin to Tacoma through a telephone number for one of his old girlfriends. The two young people were still in touch, and the girl knew John was doing autocad work (electronic drafting) for an engineering company near Seattle-Tacoma International Airport.

Stogsdill, Branchflower, and a Washington State Trooper

went to young Carlin's workplace in early May of 2005. They asked about Carlin at the front desk, hoping to meet in an office or conference room, but the firm's receptionist asked them to wait while she fetched him. Young John met the officers in the waiting room. They invited him outside and did the interview under a tree in a corner of the parking lot. Stogsdill said they did not record the interview because they were near a main highway and under the SeaTac flight path, which would have caused noise interference. Instead they simply talked and—after the interview—drove to a nearby lot and hurriedly took notes while their memories were still fresh.

Stogsdill said the young man seemed shaken by the interview. He smoked cigarettes incessantly and the words tumbled rapidly. He couldn't get the story out fast enough. (He would later tell Mechele that the officers "sweated" the story out of him. He would also testify in his father's trial that there were no loud noises near where he worked, contradicting statements by the three officers who interviewed him.)

Young Carlin reported, among other things, that his father had purchased a Desert Eagle .44 magnum shortly after the family arrived in Alaska, that the seller was a man who came to the house, and that after the shooting of Kent Leppink, he saw his father washing the pistol in bleach in a bathroom sink.

John said he was preparing to walk his dog one morning and pulled a leash from the closet. The leash snagged on a plastic bag, which fell heavily to the floor. It contained the pistol. The boy said he picked it up, looked in the bag and handled the gun. His father shortly afterward took it from him and washed the pistol in bleach, presumably to remove fingerprints from it.

Young Carlin also told detectives that his father explained that washing the gun with a caustic solution like bleach was a good way to get rid of evidence. (That seemed a strange thing for a man to say to his son, if in fact he said it, but this case

Dead Man's Dancer 61

involved many strange things.)

When Branchflower returned to Alaska with Stogsdill, she went to the Anchorage Daily News and requested access to its file of old newspapers. Since the boy said his father bought the Desert Eagle shortly after the family's arrival in Alaska, that narrowed the search. Though more than 11 years had passed since the pistol's purchase, Branchflower found the classified ad in less than two hours. It was a classified that ran in the Sunday newspaper on January 29, 1995, and offered a .44 Desert Eagle with holster and belt, three clips, ammunition, carrying case and paperwork, "$850 or best offer."

The phone number in the ad was obsolete, but telephone company records led them to an Air Force enlisted man in Arizona who had been stationed at Elmendorf Air Force Base in Anchorage from 1991-1998. The airman said he had sold a Desert Eagle to a man in South Anchorage in 1995. Detectives showed him a photo of the elder Carlin, but the airman didn't recognize him. He said the room in the background of the photograph, especially its bookcase, looked familiar, but not the face. The airman said the man he sold the gun to was burly and in his early 30s, a fair description of Kent Leppink as well as Carlin.

The laptop computer was another loose end. Alaska State Troopers were still holding it even though Mechele stopped cooperating with them as a result, saying she wanted it back before she would help them anymore. Sergeant DeHart had talked to the Leppink family in November, 1996, seven months after the murder, and asked if they would give up their claim to the laptop if it would mean greater cooperation by Mechele. They agreed, but when DeHart next talked to her the following January, Mechele thought the officer hemmed and hawed about the computer issue, so she stopped cooperating altogether. DeHart was reluctant to part with the laptop until the case was resolved, so it remained in the trooper evidence locker until Detective Branchflower had it removed and turned over—with Carlin's desktop computer—to computer forensics experts working with the Cold Case unit.

CHAPTER 16
The Arrests

Stogsdill, Branchflower, and the state's Cold Case legal team took their collection of evidence to an Alaska grand jury in early fall of 2006. Though that evidence was largely circumstantial—in fact there was still no direct evidence linking either Mechele or Carlin to the crime—the testimony of young John Carlin was enough to convince the grand jurors that the total weight of the evidence supported the case that the two had conspired to kill Kent Leppink. Both Mechele Linehan, as she was then known, and John Carlin were charged with conspiracy and first-degree murder.

Carlin's list of people to call if he was arrested was still in a briefcase of his papers ten years after he left Alaska. Carlin was then 49 and working for the New Jersey Department of Transportation in Elmer when he learned that an Alaska grand jury had indicted him and Alaska State Troopers held a warrant charging him with first-degree murder. He flew back to Anchorage and turned himself in at the Anchorage courthouse. The briefcase was turned over to police in New Jersey by Carlin's second wife, a Russian medical worker he met online. She divorced him shortly after the arrest.

Carlin had a statue of two deer that he kept on his fireplace mantle, but his wife had always felt it didn't go with the decor of the house. After he headed back to Anchorage, she put it up for sale on eBay. The ad was spotted by New Jersey police, who came for it. Engraved on the statue's bottom was Kent Leppink's name.

The charges against John Carlin and Mechele Linehan became public in early October, 2006, after the grand jury completed its review of the evidence and formally indicted the pair.

CHAPTER 17
The Carlin Trial Opens

When Carlin went to trial in March 2007, the Anchorage courtroom was jammed with lawyers, spectators, and an international corps of news media. The case drew wide attention both because of Mechele's unique story and the film noir nature of the murder plot. The trial prosecutor claimed that Mechele and Carlin borrowed their plot from the popular movie *The Last Seduction*, in which a femme fatale convinces her lover to kill her husband for insurance money. The movie connection and Mechele's beauty drew a wide array of news cameras to the small courtroom, their operators jockeying for position.

Media interest was compounded by the finger-pointing letter written by Kent Leppink while he was still alive and pointing to Mechele and John as his likely killers should he be found dead—with Scott Hilke as a third possibility. Since no charges were brought against Hilke, the media assumed he would be only a very interesting witness.

After jury selection and administration of the oath, Judge Philip Volland gave the jurors their instructions, then turned to prosecutor Patrick Gullufsen and said, "You have the floor."

"Thank you," Gullufsen replied. "May it please the court, Madam Clerk, counsel for the defense, ladies and gentlemen of the jury. It was a little over 11 years ago, a little short of 11 years, actually, that Kent Leppink was found dead near Hope, Alaska, on a dirt road off the main highway. He had been shot three times, once in the back, once in the abdomen and once in the face on the right side of his chin.

"Now, I'm going to show some pictures right off the bat of Kent as he lay there dead. I want to prepare you for that kind of photograph without shocking you right off the bat. I think it's important for you to see where we ... where law enforcement started with this case, and where his family started with this case, and that's with Kent laying on his back on a dirt road off the Hope highway, alone and dead."

Gullufsen showed the jurors a series of gruesome crime scene photos before flashing one of Kent and Mechele on the courtroom screen, a shot taken in 1995 at Elevation 92, an Anchorage restaurant.

"Now, what we're going to do in this case, ladies and gentlemen, is take a long journey through the evidence that's going to give us a lot of answers about how Kent went from someone who was alive . . . able to get up and face each day, no matter what it was going to bring, into somebody whose life was gone because he was shot and left alone on a dirt road near Hope.

"The evidence isn't going to give you all the answers, but when you've heard it all and we've examined it all, had a chance to explore it with each other, there will be no reasonable doubt that John Carlin, as an accessory or as a principal, was responsible for the murder of Kent Leppink.

"It's a story that's going to involve passion, greed, manipulation and deception, and it's those explosive forces and the actions of Carlin and of Mechele Hughes that just exploded on Kent Leppink in late April of 1996 and led to his death."

Gullufsen, a specialist in Cold Case prosecutions, gave a

summary narrative of Mechele's various romances and the events that brought her together with Carlin, Kent, Hilke, and Reddell. He showed the jurors a plastic replica of a Desert Eagle .44 magnum and ran through a preview of what the various witnesses would say, including the insurance man who sold Kent the million-dollar policy on his life, and the circumstances around the murder and the initial investigation.

Gullufsen summarized the roles of the various players in the drama. "First," he said, "Kent Leppink. The evidence will indicate that Kent was basically viewed as—at least with respect to Mechele—as kind of a houseboy that would do anything for her and was used in that fashion by her and many of the others in the household.

"Scott Hilke, you will see and hear, was somewhat more arrogant. He looked down on the other people. It would appear that if there was anybody that Ms. Hughes was really enamored with, it would have been Mr. Hilke. Mr. Hilke did not have the money to spend on her that the others did, and did not, so far as we know. He used a lot of mileage he had built up to transport her around, however.

"Mr. Carlin was the quiet one, the observant one, the smart one, the one with money. Mr. Reddell, as I've indicated, pretty much was not in the picture …. Ms. Hughes has been indicted as well for her responsibility in the death of Mr. Leppink …. [Y]ou're going to be called upon to make determinations in this case about what her role was in various aspects of this case …. and in Mr. Leppink's murder. What you're being asked to do in this case is to determine Mr. Carlin's guilt or innocence. Another (trial) like this will make that determination as to Ms. Hughes."

Defense attorney Marcy McDannel took her first try at diverting attention from her client and laying the blame on Mechele during her opening statement. "Now, I predict as the trial goes along and you start to see the full scope of the evidence, all the parties involved, everyone that Mechele Hughes managed to tangle into her web of deception and greed and manipulation that she was weaving back in '95 and '96, that this is going to become a very engrossing question for you, because I think you're going to find that it's something that just cannot be solved.

"But, ladies and gentlemen ... I want to stress to you that's not going to be our job in this case. Our job is going to be to determine whether or not the state has the evidence to prove that the man they've put on trial for first degree murder, Mr. John Carlin over here, did they have the evidence to prove that he had anything to do with the death of Kent Leppink."

McDannel argued that the state's contention that Carlin was part of a love triangle involving Carlin, the victim Kent, and Mechele was an overly simplistic and unlikely explanation of what happened. She said the state should also be considering other possible suspects in the shooting like Hilke, Carlin's son John, Brett Reddell, and perhaps Mechele herself.

In detailing the many expensive gifts Mechele received from her suitors, McDannel referred to several fur coats given to her. "I believe we will see many, many receipts from David Green Furriers," she said, "indicating that Mechele was not going to go cold in the winter."

McDannel said Carlin and Kent were pretty much in the same boat since they had given Mechele expensive gifts and they were friends, but they were both well aware that Hilke had won her heart. She said Carlin had told police that if he was going to kill anybody, it would have been Hilke.

She added that the highly publicized Hope note—written by Mechele and Carlin to convince Kent she was in Hope—was not drafted in a way that would allow him to be ambushed. It contained no directions to Carlin's cabin and said only that it was in Hope, a fairly large area, mostly forested. The ambiguous wording suggested strongly that the note was, in fact, intended only to keep Kent from tracking Mechele and Scott to their trysting place at Lake Tahoe by throwing him off their trail.

McDannel noted that nothing happened to Kent while Mechele was in California and Carlin was in Anchorage. Kent was killed after Mechele returned. And, though the window of opportunity in which Mechele could have killed Kent was only nine-and-a-half hours, it could have been time enough. She said it was also possible that Hilke returned to Anchorage with Mechele and participated in the murder, but police apparently didn't check Hilke's travel records to be sure one way or the other.

McDannel said Mechele was juggling a complex mix of deceits, keeping her various relationships from her several lovers and fiancés. "I mean, the amount of juggling that she can do is extensive. She's manipulative, greedy, and you're going to hear from several witnesses, I expect, including her own sister, that she ... has an explosive temper when she's crossed. People don't do what she wants them to do, she explodes."

The defense lawyer said Mechele had so many love affairs going, so many triangles, that it was far too simplistic to assume that John Carlin killed Kent Leppink or to rule out the possibility that Mechele acted alone. "Ladies and gentlemen, this is a case that frankly cannot be solved and certainly cannot be proved beyond a reasonable doubt with respect to Mr. Carlin, no way, not even close. You will not get past a maybe, and that's why I will ask you to find him not guilty. Thank you."

The first witness was Mike Gephardt, the Chugach Electric supervisor who first spotted Kent's body on the power line trail outside Hope. Gephardt recounted his discovery that day and his assistance to the State Troopers as they arrived on the scene.

Gephardt was followed on the witness stand by Dr. Norman Thompson, the pathologist who examined Kent's body in the Anchorage morgue. Dr. Thompson described what he found when he cut open the body and examined its internal organs and the contents of the detailed report he gave detectives. Thompson said the victim's three bullet wounds told much about what happened that day in the forest. The first bullet was in the back, just to the right of the body midline and directed slightly upward, exiting from his stomach. The shot appeared to have been taken on a slope by a gunman behind and slightly below the victim, who then fell forward into a depression in the trail.

Thompson said gases driven into Kent's body from the gun's muzzle indicated that when the trigger was pulled the pistol was pressed against the victim's back, perhaps even poking into his back. The first shot's impact spun him around and knocked him to the ground, mortally wounded and facing his killer.

The second shot was in the stomach a little above the bellybutton, at a sharp upward angle. The exit wound for that bullet was high on the back. The lack of significant blood on the front of the victim's T-shirt, nearest the second bullet wound, indicated he was lying on his back and moved very little, if at all, after the first shot.

The third bullet struck Kent in the right chin, at an angle right to left. It also was fired from extreme close range, perhaps a few inches to two feet away, stippling his face with unburned gunpowder. Thompson testified that each of the three shots would have been fatal even without the other two bullets. Kent was dying after the first and had virtually no blood pressure left by the time the third was fired. He was near death and probably

Dead Man's Dancer   71

not struggling when the third shot hit him in the face.[4]

Dr. Thompson said the body may have been lying there for a day or two—or longer—before being found.

The expert witness list also included Robert Shem, ballistics man at the Alaska Crime Lab. The day after Kent's body was discovered, while Dr. Thompson was conducting the autopsy, Shem inspected the three spent cartridge cases and the bullets and fragments taken from the body. Shem testified that the shells were definitely from a .44 magnum weapon, presumably a pistol.[5]

Shem confirmed the bullets bore the unique rifling marks of a Desert Eagle automatic. The ballistics expert also looked at a holster retrieved from Mechele's car. He said he used a scalpel to open the seams and look at wear patterns inside. The holster had been most often used to carry a Desert Eagle.

Others on the witness list included the State Trooper Cold Case investigators, a computer expert, the cook at the Discovery Cafe in Hope, an employee of the insurance company office, lawyer Brian Brundin, members of the Leppink family, Scott Hilke, Carlin's Russian wife Carla, and a New Jersey State Police detective who retrieved Kent Leppink's deer statue from Carla Carlin. Also, the previous owner of the Desert Eagle .44, the jeweler who sold Kent and Carlin the diamonds they gave Mechele, plus Mechele's sister Melissa, Carlin's son John Carlin IV, and Adella Perez, young John's ex-girlfriend.

The most damning testimony came from young Carlin, who said that a few days after the murder he came around a

---

[4] A psychoanalyst who reviewed the evidence at the request of the author reported the third shot in the face suggests the shooter was very angry with Kent. In the vernacular of television, the first and second bullets could be considered business, the business of killing the victim, but the third was strictly personal.

[5] The .44 magnum cartridge is used in some rifles, but the slug is large and relatively slow, best used in short-range hunting, as is common in deer country. Though handguns are common, rifles in .44 magnum are rarely seen in Alaska, where distances are often long. And .44 magnum automatic pistols are rarer still.

corner at his family's Anchorage home and saw his father and Mechele near a bathroom sink half-filled with bleach. He said he saw a pistol in the sink soaking in the bleach.

When the younger Carlin was cross-examined by his father's defense attorney Sidney Billingslea, she suggested that he himself might have been the one who shot Kent Leppink. Billingslea said documents filed in the case indicated that he was in fact considered a suspect. Carlin's other defense lawyer, Marcy McDannel, also discussed in her argument the possibility that the Carlin boy was the shooter. The defense suggested that the jury consider young Carlin as an alternate suspect, but, with no convincing evidence to implicate him, the issue was not pursued.

Search warrants sought by State Troopers early in the case did list young Carlin as a suspect in the case, but investigators dismissed the implication that he was under suspicion for the murder itself. They said the implication of guilt was simply a poor choice of words in writing the warrant request.

Later in the trial, lawyer Billingslea countered that the younger Carlin was in fact a suspect because he had motive, means and opportunity to kill Kent Leppink. Billingslea also asked young Carlin, apparently at the suggestion of his father, whether he said on the day Kent disappeared, "I've got to get that guy out of here."[6]

One day as the trial dragged on, Mechele walked past Carlin IV outside the courthouse. Though her husband tried to talk her out of it, she impulsively ran up to the youth and gave him a big hug. Afterward she turned and walked away, wiping tears from her eyes.

Though the trooper case against John Carlin depended very much on the veracity of his son, a number of people, including

---

[6] Detective Jim Stogsdill said in an interview after the trial that he and his Cold Case team never ruled young Carlin out as a suspect, but they felt the evidence pointing toward the elder Carlin and Mechele was so strong that they considered the boy an unlikely candidate as the shooter.

Dead Man's Dancer

young John's former girlfriend Adella Perez, considered the boy a compulsive liar. The Perez girl testified that she started dating young John shortly after his mother died in the spring of 1995. At that time, she said, he seemed introverted and very intelligent, though "a little bizarre at times." As the months went on the boy became increasingly volatile and prone to eruptions of temper.

Perez said John IV smashed his hand against his car twice and another time into a wall in the house, leaving a hole in the drywall. He was terrified about what his father might do when he saw the wall damage, to an extent that surprised Adella. She and John patched the wall with plaster and used pasta seasoning to give it an aged look matching the wall. The patch and cover-up job were effective, but the incident left Adella troubled by the boy's fear of his father's wrath.

She said that on another occasion young John picked up his family dog without reason or warning, carried it out on a second-floor balcony and dropped it over the side. The animal landed on a couch on the deck below, frightened but apparently unhurt. Adella added that, in the last few months she dated him, young John became increasingly homophobic, was hanging around with a crowd using marijuana and LSD, and became jealous of anyone who tried to get close to her. He seemed to get weirder as time went on, with John occasionally "tweaking out." The changes in his personality and her concerns about them led eventually to their breakup.

Adella said she moved to California at the end of 1995, but she and John stayed in touch by telephone. Both were talkers and the conversations were long. They missed each other and John was unhappy in school, making him wish he was with her. She would tell him about her new life in the Golden State, her new friends and school there.

After Kent was killed, Adella and young John discussed the

murder. Adella knew that John and Kent had previously seemed close—often playing games on Kent's laptop computer—and had been living together in the same house, but John seemed surprisingly unconcerned about his friend's death.

Glib and intelligent, John Carlin IV had the language skills of a lawyer, though his formal education largely ceased after high school. He also claimed to have a memory that would recall whether or not his dog woke him 11 years earlier when a garage door opened in the family's Anchorage home the day Kent Leppink was killed. The boy's bedroom was over the garage. He said the dog would wake him when the garage door opened beneath them. When the prosecutor in his father' case asked if the dog woke him the morning of the murder, the boy said it did not.

A neighbor testified she was looking out the window of her home a few weeks after the murder when she saw young John Carlin staring at her from a window in his father's home. Shortly afterward she saw the boy climb out on the roof of his house and retrieve something from the gutter, then hastily climb back through a window. The item recovered was never identified.

CHAPTER 18
Email

The heart of the government's case was revealed when Alaska State Trooper Christopher Thompson took the stand. Thompson was the computer expert who examined Carlin's desktop and the laptop jointly owned by Kent Leppink and Mechele Hughes. Thompson used forensic software to read and copy messages that had been "deleted" from the computers. Only the markers that prevent the computer from writing over information remaining on the hard drive correspondence were gone. The underlying emails were intact.

The messages told an intriguing story of the Carlin household in the last few months of Kent's life. Many discussions could be interpreted either as a murder plot in the works or something else entirely, perhaps simply a household in turmoil and coming apart at the seams.

Most of the email messages submitted with the prosecution's evidence didn't seem to indicate much except the growing infatuation both Kent and John Carlin had with Mechele. They did, however, provide valuable insight into what was happening.

In one from Super Bowl weekend in January, 1996, Scott Hilke is at a convention in Phoenix and anxious to get back to Mechele in Anchorage. She has quit her job at The Bush

Company and is taking classes at the University of Alaska Anchorage. He wishes she could have come with him to Phoenix but acknowledges that studying must come first.

Other comments in the emails indicated both Kent and Carlin were snooping on Mechele as their passion for her increased. Kent began by reading her email, then graduated to reading credit card bills and telephone records for both Mechele and Hilke (and probably Carlin, as well). Carlin apparently limited his own spying to reading Mechele's email. He did it so often that in late February she got a new email address, switching most of her email traffic from the username 'Akmewell' to 'latexnlace.' She told Hilke about the new name in a message on February 27.

"jon has my passwrd for akmewell," she wrote. "send email to new name latexnlace. I dont want to change password right now. he almost saw last leter. Jon is coming up now hav to go love you always will rite later."[7]

The next day Hilke wrote back to Mechele saying that strange things were happening with the new email address, perhaps indicating yet more snooping.

"Something very fishy going on here," he said. "I am forwarding email recieved yesterday as well as replies. The letter asking questions for security purposes was read @ 11:20 a.m Tuesday, your time. The name 'Latexnlace' is no longer recognized as a user. Was it you or is it someone invading? Please answer the questions re: cousins and street in your next email so I know it's you and we can figure out a better security system."

---

[7] The email contained many misspellings and grammatical errors, which Mechele told the author resulted from hurried writing. She said the often sloppy email was caused by the marginally reliable computer equipment available at the time. They were using dial-up modems, to old-fashioned telephone lines and were subject to unexpected lost signals. "We had to hurry or we'd get kicked off," she said. The result was semi-garbled messages resembling many of today's Twitter tweets.

Dead Man's Dancer

The problem he complained about may have been related to launching a new email moniker with America Online, but snooping into email files by both Kent and Carlin, and unauthorized opening of messages, generated increasing fury in the already agitated household. The fuse in the explosive Carlin house smoldered on.

On March 10, Kent sent an email to Hilke complaining about efforts by Hilke and Mechele to hide their relationship from him. "You and Mechele hurt me very much," he wrote. The note—written while Kent was still in the midst of planning a wedding for himself and Mechele—was conciliatory and said he understood how Hilke felt about her. He felt the same way. And he wanted Hilke to be his friend despite their rivalry.

"From the moment I first suspected that there might be something going on between you and Mechele, I should have said something. By remaining silent, I am as guilty as you. . . . By being silent, bad feelings towards you developed. I keep too much inside, and all the pressures build up until the only thing that is left is resentment.

"I would have to say that I put up a pretty good false front, but on the inside, I was a bundle of mixed up emotions: desire for love, hatred, bitterness, confusion ... Mechele and I have talked a lot in the past few days, and I am drawing a line and putting all of this behind me. I am not putting this in the back of my brain so that I can pull it up whenever I want to . . . I am not going to ever bring it up again. I think a clean slate is the best way to continue. I want to be your friend. I don't want any bad feelings about the past to interfere with our friendship.

"From here on out, a new beginning. It makes me feel good to call you my friend. Let's get together soon. Or at least keep in touch by email.

TT"

CHAPTER 19
A Wedding Present

The recovered electronic messages showed Mechele continued her affair with Scott Hilke even while she and Kent made plans for what Kent expected to be their wedding.

In an email on March 17, Carlin told Mechele he was giving up his own hope of winning her heart and acknowledged Hilke had won her. When he sent the email, Mechele was visiting Hilke in California and planning to go soon to New Orleans, though she was scheduled to return to Anchorage between the two trips. Carlin suggested Mechele stay with Hilke until it was time for her to head for Louisiana.

Carlin's recognition that he had lost the competition for Mechele's heart puts an odd twist on the police and prosecutor's belief that Kent's shooting resulted from a plot of murder for insurance money. If Carlin wasn't going to get the girl—and there is nothing to indicate his note was a ruse—then the murder and insurance payout would have been an engagement or wedding present, Carlin's going-away gift to her. Carlin was certainly still enchanted by Mechele, but the notion of the murder as a gift to his lost love requires a bizarre stretch of the imagination.

It's quite possible, of course, that they planned to split the insurance money and go their separate ways, but the bulk of the trial evidence suggests that is an unlikely conclusion. And, a cold-blooded plot in which she takes the insurance money and says goodbye would have been a sharp contrast to Carlin's passionate love for her. While possible, it seems improbable.

The March 17 email contained other unexplained references, including this mysterious one:

"I will call you when it is in," Carlin wrote, a possible reference to paperwork on the insurance policy, or to the pending check from Kent's father, or perhaps even paperwork on the bird sanctuary in Costa Rica.

"It doesn't make sense to come up here unless it is ready; it cannot be rushed. You just have to wait for it to come in. You can also take care of it by mail. You don't even have to be here. I will still take care of my end.

"It is clear to me that Scott wants you to move to CA with him and that is why you got a ticket for one month. We have said that we would be honest with each other and keep no secrets. I am living up to my end, as are you. It is probably better for you to be in CA as you don't like Alaska that much and you do like Scott. I am a business partner and must be content with that role …. Scott is a lucky man, a real lucky man …. Please be well, safe, and happy. I love you more than life. I love you more than that. With all of my love that I have to offer you, John"

The reference to Mechele and Carlin as business partners suggests they might have been buying the bird sanctuary together, which might or might not mean they planned to kill Kent for the insurance money.

In another email that same day, the lovelorn steelworker asked Mechele, "When Scott asks you to move in with him, and we both know that he will, are you going to?"

Her answer, if she gave one, probably came in one of her many telephone calls from travel spots back to the Carlin household. How much Carlin and Kent did their own talking with her via phone is unknown, but when pouring their heart out to her they seemed to prefer the relative privacy of email. Often they would raise questions or issues via email—each hiding their writings from the other—and she would respond verbally when she called them, leaving an incomplete and tantalizing record.

Since Carlin sometimes used his computer to explore the Gaymall website, he and Mechele at times used its confidential mail system to communicate without having Kent find their messages. In an undated email from him to her, he describes his pleasure at logging on to Gaymall and finding a message from Mechele, who is in the house with Carlin but using the computer to avoid being overheard. He also describes growing frustration with Kent's obtrusive presence in the household.

"This atmosphere here is very unhealthy," Carlin wrote, "and I will never have a fair shot at winning your heart and love. It frustrates me so much. Kent is here. He is very weird. He interceeds in any time I might have with you. I cannot openly talk to you, as he might hear. I cannot interact with you because he is here. I know that you don't want to come to Alaska anymore. It is easy to tell that .... If I were you, I would dread coming to this house right now. It cannot be any fun for you. I blame it on Kent and feel that I am paying the price for this. If he were not here, we could sit on the couch and just talk. We could talk at the table over dinner. We could become closer instead of further apart, which is what is happening, without the communication that is necessary. We will never get close when we must sneak around to have a five-minute talk or just hold hands.

"This atmosphere is just so unhealthy for a relationship. I get so frustrated, I don't want to wait, just do it now. But our future is at stake and I am forced to wait .... Please remind me of the errands that must be taken care of with Kent. There are things that must be done. With all the love I have to give you, John"

The undated message seemed very suspicious and appeared to refer to Carlin's plans for Kent, which could have meant his murder. But the fact that it contained no date and said, "our future is at stake," suggests that it was written sometime before Carlin gave up his hope of winning Mechele, or, if his abandonment of hope was a pretense, before the pretense began.

CHAPTER 20
When Kent Met Mechele

The emails discovered by Trooper Thompson showed that on March 10, Kent wrote to Carlin, a long, rambling missive apparently resulting both from his own desire to bare his feelings and Carlin's statement that he wanted more email. In it he tells of meeting Mechele for the first time, their initial romance and engagement.

Kent's first trip to The Bush Company was during a birthday celebration for a friend named Bryan. They were drinking heavily at seats front and center on the "meat rack," an unadorned dancing stage with seats around the perimeter. There men showed appreciation for the beauty and performances of the scantily clad dancers by placing money on the edge of the stage. When a musical number ended, the dancers would scoop up the money and drop by a donor's barstool or table to offer a lap dance.

"We were getting pretty lubricated," Kent wrote, "when Bryan turned to me and made the comment that the best-looking woman at the Bush was walking down the stairs. It happened to be Mechele, and she was coming onstage. When she danced for us, I whispered in her ear that I would like her to do a table dance—on me—for Bryan for his birthday."

Kent wrote that his friend returned from his table dance—

performed in a quiet corner of the club's main room—and kept raving about how great she was. So Kent bought Bryan another up close and personal dance by Mechele. When the friend returned still talking about her, Kent decided to see this female phenomenon for himself. He stopped buying dances for Bryan and focused his own attentions on the attractive young woman. Kent quickly learned what many Bush Company customers already knew—that the woman they knew as Bobby Joe was a much better conversationalist than a dancer. Though her dancing consisted mostly of rhythmical wiggling, she was charming and often won the hearts of the men she met; they opened their wallets just to keep her talking at their tables.

Before the night ended, Kent bravely ventured to ask the young woman for a date on the following Saturday afternoon— and she accepted. As they left the club that night, Kent told Bryan he intended to marry her.

Kent and his new love dated several times—he by then knew that her real name was Mechele Hughes—and he became a regular at the Bush Company, staring dazed at the various ladies of the meat rack almost every night, waiting for Mechele's appearance.

The fisherman kept the relationship with Mechele going by handing over large amounts of cash, about $10,000 in the first month. "That's a pretty dear sum for a deckhand to be forking out," he wrote to Carlin, "but I knew what I wanted."

When she told Kent she was trying to put money together to buy a house, he gave her $500 toward the down payment and $600 for closing costs. He fantasized the house would one day be their first honeymoon cottage and their home.

Shortly afterward, Mechele flew to New Orleans for a vacation with her family. When she returned and found her new house not ready, Kent invited her to stay with him in his apartment. Mechele declined so he rented a room in the Sheraton Anchorage

Hotel for several nights. He slept chastely in a chair while she used the bed. They talked about their future life together, having children and deferring sex until after the wedding.

Kent had already purchased an engagement ring and formally asked her to marry him on Nov. 14, 1994. They decided to wait and set a date later, but in the meantime Mechele needed a few things—a new Jeep to replace her Volvo, a washing machine, refrigerator and miscellaneous items for the house.

Kent decided she needed everything on her list, including the Jeep, even though her Volvo was only a few years old. The Jeep's rugged construction and four-wheel drive would be very appropriate for Alaska's back country, though Mechele showed no sign of interest in the Alaska wilderness. He didn't have enough money to buy everything on the list and decided to call on his father in Michigan, who had promised each of his sons $15,000 in an interest-free loan when they decided to buy houses. Kent asked his father for $10,000 and used it to buy Mechele the things she wanted.

Kent said in the email to Carlin that, shortly after he began dating Mechele, the first dark cloud swept in over the relationship. He said Mechele assured him that Scott Hilke was gay and no threat to their relationship, even though Hilke had quit his job and was moving to Alaska. Kent was suspicious and doubted the claim about Hilke having no sexual interest in her.

"Call me stupid," he wrote, "but for quite a while I didn't see any problem. It should have hit me as strange that Mechele never woke up but that she called up Scott to see what was up. At night she had to call to see what he had done that day. Every time she would fly out of state, she would somehow meet up with Scott, and spend some time together. Hawaii, Florida, California, New Orleans, Seattle."

Speaking of himself in the third person and using his

Dead Man's Dancer

nickname, Kent wrote, "99.9 percent of the population knows what's up by now, but not TT. All he knows is what Mechele has told him, and he loves her more than anything. Why would he think anything was going on?

"Well, TT finally catches on when he finds some faxes that are left out. You didn't have to read between the lines to know what they were saying. Scott asked Mechele to marry him on November 24, 1994, ten days after I had.

"There's no way to describe my feelings, John. I guess I was as mad at myself as I was at Scott and Mechele. So what did I do? I still loved Mechele. I couldn't leave her; she meant too much to me. I guess I did the only sensible thing. I slowed down the flow of money. I couldn't see giving my money to Mechele when I knew it was really going to Scott so that he could fuck around and not work and vacation away a summer with the woman that I love and .... It was really fucking up my head to know the whole situation and yet not have the balls enough to confront the problem."

Kent said he knew Hilke and Mechele had broken up several times and that the relationship was taking a toll on her. He was relieved when the two seemed to drift apart, but then Carlin himself became a rival for Mechele's affections.

Mechele had told him that Carlin was just a customer and a friend, not serious competition for her love. She told Kent once more that he was her boyfriend, not Carlin. "Here we go again," Kent wrote to Carlin.

The email indicated Kent and Carlin had some kind of air-clearing conversation a few nights earlier, involving some rare frank discussions. "We should have talked sooner," he said. "Let's not close down the communications we've got open now. If something is bothering us, let's talk about it."

Carlin replied saying he would keep Kent's secrets and urged him not to worry about losing Mechele's heart.

"I have kept many secrets from Mechele that Scott has asked me to keep," Carlin wrote to Kent. "Mechele knows that I have those secrets, and I have told her that I won't tell her. I told Scott I would not repeat those conversations/secrets. Scott, however, told her bits of those conversations, which made me look like a smacked ass. I still did not betray my word.... I don't know why you worried about me. I'm a fat, bald man with no social graces. You know my medical problems and I don't need to go into it. Our friendship is unique. It is also safe from emotional romance but not from loyalty to her from friendship ... Your friend, John."

On March 11, Kent wrote another long email to Carlin. He asked that Carlin read it as often as he wanted, then delete it and not say a word to anyone. He said he promised Mechele that he wouldn't talk about such things again. Speaking once more of his love at first sight, Kent adds, "It would seem pretty strange to say that, knowing where she used to work, but when she would do table dances for me, I was watching her eyes. Sure, it's hard not to see the naked body in front of you, but I felt more for her than just as a sex object."

Kent described how disillusioned he was when he learned that Scott Hilke wasn't gay and that the salesman and Mechele were having a steamy love affair. "You have nothing to worry about," she had told him.

"And I really didn't worry about it. I'm supposed to trust the one I love, and believe everything she says. I invested a lot more than just money in this relationship. I invested my time and my emotions, the latter being something I consider to be more valuable than any amount of money."

Kent said he realized Mechele and Hilke had called off their own wedding plans when he returned to Anchorage after the

Dead Man's Dancer

1995 fishing season. But then he realized Mechele was also engaged to marry Carlin and that devastated him once again.[8]

"I didn't know what I had done wrong. Or if I had done anything wrong. I wondered about sex. You know where I stand on sex, and I was wondering if because we hadn't had a sexual relationship that Mechele was going to go out and find it somewhere else .... I don't go to doctors, not until I've cut something off that needs to be sewn back on, so it was difficult for me to go to the shrink. I don't think I'll be going again. He wasn't worth a shit, as I figured, but he was a warm body. A live human who I could let everything out with, and that really helped."

An undated email found on the same portion of the laptop hard drive was from Kent to Mechele. The fisherman said he used the computer as a primary means of communication with her and his few friends because, "I can express myself better in text than I can in conversation, especially on delicate subjects.

"On our wedding night, I'll be giving myself to you, and not before. I love you so much. Our lust for each other is healthy, not a handicap. Your weakness is my strength and vice versa .... If your sex drive is one hundredth of what mine is, you would have had your legs spread wide begging me to be inside of you had I actually wanted to. But I didn't and I won't let that happen.

"I want right now to be able to hold you, to caress you, to kiss you. I'm not asking you to walk around naked and all. Let's try and keep our nudity to a minimum until we are married. I'm not embarrassed to be naked around you. In fact, I enjoy it more than being clothed. And I'm not embarrassed about you being naked around me. But could we keep it to a

---

[8] Kent was unique in his naive emotions toward Mechele. She considered all three of her fiancées to be "marks," privileged customers whose relationships with her extended beyond her workplace. Carlin and Hilke more or less understood and reluctantly accepted the tenuous relationship and the place in her life of the others. Each managed to convince himself he was special, and Mechele encouraged that belief, but Mechele seemed to consider them all customers who just happened to be enchanted with her.

minimum until the wedding. It's almost like knowing what the present is before you open it.

"Also, I would appreciate it if you would make sure that top and bottom have clothes on when you walk around the house any more. You are going to be my wife, and nobody else's. Call me selfish, but so far as your breasts and pussy are concerned, I want to be the only person that looks at them. You are the only person I let see my penis. And you will always be the only person. End of lecture.

"I want to let you know that I don't think any differently of you because you aren't a virgin. You did what you did because you are you. We can't change the past, nor would I want to. But I will never hold it against you because we are virgins. Since we will not make love until we are married, we as a couple will be virgins, and that means a lot to me.

"Last night you said something that I have been feeling for some time. You asked me if we could fly away to Reno and get married. You wouldn't have said that if you weren't feeling it. My reply: YES! Let's go now. I want to marry you and start a family. The one thing that I would ask is that our parents be there. I want us all to be a family, and I don't want to have your mother miss her daughter's wedding. My mother would kill me if I didn't let her come to our wedding. Let's talk on this seriously! All my love ... Kent"

The elopement never took place.

CHAPTER 21
Amateur Sleuthing

Carlin's comments about Kent and his growing impatience would weigh on the jurors' minds. The comment " … just do it now," suggests Carlin wanted to get on with the murder, though the words were vague enough to leave other possibilities as well.

"Please remind me of the errands that must be taken care of with Kent. There are things that must be done," suggests Mechele and Carlin were planning something with regard to Carlin's problem tenant. But what?

Perhaps a checklist of things to do before the killing?

In another email from Mechele to Carlin, she said that after Kent left to go fishing in May, she did not want him to move back into the house with them again. That could mean either that she wanted him dead or simply did not want him allowed back into the house.

Both Mechele and Carlin began to wonder just how much Kent knew, how many of their messages he had read. Kent's amateur detective work put all three of them into the sleuthing business. Kent's snooping was especially irritating to Mechele, and Carlin found that she was doing some snooping of her own, going into his email account on AOL either to read his mail or see what might have been read illicitly by Kent. In an electronic note on March 30, after she returned to Anchorage,

Carlin told her that when he tried to sign on to his AOL account, he received a message indicating that he was already signed on.

Rather than get angry, he wrote her saying, "You are welcome to go through my AOL whenever you wish. No apologies are needed or expected. I know you have my password and knew you would use it .... I expected you to go into it when you were in California."

Amid the concern about Kent's stumbling through their email—and while Mechele was telling Carlin she didn't want Kent back in the house after fishing season—Mechele continued to encourage Kent on their wedding plans and to fan his ardor. In a March 31 note she assured him she loved him and was not procrastinating about their wedding. If, in fact, Mechele and Carlin were plotting Kent's murder while she was also planning her marriage to the victim, the venture was extraordinarily cold-blooded.

"I am just concerned that everything will be rushed," Kent wrote to Mechele, "and it worries me because I will only have one [wedding] and you know I want it to be perfect. You give me an unbinding love that is truly from your heart and everyone can see it. Many saw it way before I really knew. I knew you cared but I didn't know how much. I didn't know it had no boundaries and I hope I can make you a happy husband. I will try my hardest to keep our family strong lovin ...." (The message ends there, perhaps because the forensic recovery was unable to capture more.)

Then Mechele sent a note to Scott Hilke on March 31 saying she had or was about to come into a financial bonanza. "Hi, how is my baby? Well, I got the $ for Costa Rica. Just don't pee your pants, OK? I almost did. Let's do it. Why not? We don't have to move there now. Later, maybe." (The reference to Mechele coming into money was unexplained, unless she was thinking about Kent's expected life insurance payout. But, she seems extraordinarily cheerful for reporting of a bonanza based on a murder plot.)

On April 2 Mechele blew up at Kent and sent him a long, all-caps (the email equivalent of yelling) missive. She said she loved him, but, "PLEASE STOP SNOOPING AND ASKING ALL OF THOSE QUESTIONS. I AM SERIOUSLY TELLING YOU THIS. IF YOU CONTINUE TO RUMMAGE THROUGH MY PRIVACY AND SNOOP THROUGH MY BELONGINGS, I WILL NOT MARRY YOU. WHILE WE ARE NOT MARRIED, NOTHING IS YOURS. DO YOU GET IT?... WHEN YOU GO THROUGH MY PURSE AND MY BAGS AND MY COMPUTER, YOU ARE INVADING MY PRIVACY AND I WILL NOT TOLERATE IT."

One of the things that infuriated her was finding his personal phone book, which included names and phone numbers of some of her Bush Company clients, including one that she referred to in her own notes as "Elvis." "I KNOW THAT [name withheld] DOES NOT ALLOW YOU TO CALL HIM ELVIS AND I BET YOU WOULD NOT EVEN KNOW WHY WE CALL HIM THAT."

By this time, both Mechele and Hilke suspected that Kent was stealing things from them and hiding them in various places. The missing items included a small handgun that Hilke gave to Mechele for self-protection.

"I LOVE YOU AND YOU NEED TO KNOW THAT YOU HAVE REALLY BEEN PISSING ME OFF," she wrote. "YOU HIDE SO MUCH SHIT FROM ME. HOW DARE YOU QUESTION ME. YOUR SAFETY DEPOSIT BOXES, YOUR HIDDEN SHIT, YOUR STORAGE SHED AND ETC., ETC., ETC. I NEVER PRY INTO YOUR STORAGE. THAT WAS STEALING AND IF YOU WANT ME TO MARRY YOU ON THE 19TH THEN YOU NEED TO REALIZE I LET THAT

GO. YOU STOLE FROM ME AND I DID YOU WRONG TOO. YOU CONTINUE TO SNOOP AND PRY. STOP IF YOU WANT ME TO HAVE YOUR CHILDREN AND SPEND THE LIFE TOGETHER THAT WE HAVE TALKED ABOUT … YOU NEED TO KNOW THESE THINGS. YOU ARE VERY CLOSE TO DRIVING ME AWAY."

It's unknown what the wedding date reference was, though Kent had been trying to pin her down on a day they could get married. Mechele also indicated, again with her caps lock key firmly down, that she was anxious to get out of the Carlin house and back to her own place in Wasilla, which was still being remodeled. "I WANT TO GET OUT OF JOHN'S AND LITTLE JOHN'S LIVES AND NOT HURT EITHER ONE OF THEM. I LOVE THEM BOTH SO MUCH. I DON'T THINK YOU UNDERSTAND HOW UNHAPPY I AM THERE."

Mechele was also irritated because Kent was trying to establish a relationship with her mother, Sandy McWilliams, a realtor in South Louisiana. "STOP SENDING MY MOTHER CARDS. I DO NOT SEND HER CARDS AND YOU WON'T EITHER IF YOU ARE PART OF … PLEASE DON'T MEDDLE IN MY FAMILY RELATIONS."

A sheepish Kent responded with a long and apologetic email to her, saying he was wrong to snoop through her personal belongings. He was then in Florida visiting his own parents at their winter home and asked her to fly down and spend time with his family.

CHAPTER 22
The Wedding Gown

On April 4, Kent was preparing to go on a recreational fishing outing with his family. He recalled a compliment she gave him a few days earlier when he was back in Anchorage. "You leaned over to me and asked if I was going to get hair (he was balding). When I said no, you said, 'Good.' Then you told me I was very handsome. Nobody has ever told me that."

But the relationship between Mechele and Kent continued to blow hot and cold. She grew increasingly testy about Kent's failure to give her the $2,500 she said she needed for her wedding gown.

"I still need to get the $ for the dress," she wrote. "You said you would wire it but you have not …. It is causing me problems. When I make a promise to my grandpaw based on what you promised, I would expect you to follow through. You have not."

Mechele said Kent had told her he would wire the money to her or to Carlin, (so she could then use one of Carlin's checks), but no money had been forthcoming. "I need a definite answer or commitment," she wrote. "Now stop blowing me off and give me a definite time and place where the $ will be … Please for the sake of our marriage, tell me by 8 o'clock. – Mechele"

Kent responded with a waffling note saying he needed information about where to send the money. "Nobody has sent me any information on where the money should be sent … I don't want to make you mad or anything, but I would really like to know what the total cost of the dress is going to be. You said before that we would need about $1,000 to put down on the dress, and now you say that you need $2,500." He complained that she was leaving him out of the wedding planning process.

Mechele replied, "You were not supposed to get any info on the $. You were supposed to call John to wire it into his account."

The next day she sent another email, equally as irritated, in which she said she was about to attend a family gathering and wanted to give her grandfather his check there. She said she would not talk to Kent about anything else until the money matter was resolved. "I am pissed so do something if you love and want me as much as you say. I hope I can go pick up the $ tonight."

Kent fired back his own all-caps message, "MY PARENTS ARE PAYING FOR A LOT OF THINGS IN OUR WEDDING, AND THEY DON'T LIKE BEING LEFT OUT IN THE DARK. THEY LIKE TO KNOW WHAT EXPENSES THEY ARE GOING TO BE INCURRING BEFORE THEY HAVE TO JUST PAY FOR THINGS.

"THEY REALLY WANT TO HELP US BUT THEY DON'T WANT TO JUST HAVE A STACK OF BILLS PUT IN FRONT OF THEIR FACE AND HAVE SOMEBODY TELL THEM TO PAY THEM."

He said he would figure out for himself how to send money via Western Union, and added,

"AS FAR AS PROCRASTINATION, WHERE IS THE MONEY THAT YOU TOLD ME YOU WOULD GET TO ME FOR THE TITLE WORK AT THE HOUSE, OR FOR THE VET BILLS OR FOR THE THINGS I DID TO BRETT'S TRUCK, ETC. I ASK YOU ABOUT THE MONEY AND

Dead Man's Dancer

YOU TELL ME NOT TO WORRY ABOUT IT, THAT YOU'LL GET IT TO ME. I WAIT AND ASK AND WAIT AND ASK AND NO MONEY.

"YOU SHOW ME A PICTURE OF A BIRD CAGE AND ASK IF IT'S OK TO GET IT. THAT MAKES ME RESPONSIBLE TO PAY FOR IT? IS MY WALLET SUPPOSED TO HAVE A ONE-WAY PATH ON IT. AM I SUPPOSED TO JUST PAY BILLS AND NOT KNOW WHERE THE MONEY IS GOING TO OR HELP MAKE PLANS FOR ITS USE? I DON'T THINK SO ...

"ENOUGH OF THIS BULL SHIT! I WILL NOT ARGUE ABOUT MONEY ... I WILL BE IN ALASKA TOMORROW NIGHT AND I WILL GIVE THE MONEY TO JOHN THERE. YOU CAN WRITE ONE OF HIS CHECKS FOR IT THERE."

Kent noted that Mechele would have been angry if he had asked her for $1,000 for a deposit on his wedding tux, and simply said he'd ask for the balance when it was done. "YOU'D RAISE A SHIT FIT AND ASK WHAT THE COST WOULD BE AND WHEN IT WOULD BE DONE."

In another note, written in normal keyboard voice, Kent said he told his father that the $2,500 she wanted for her wedding gown and veil was only "a down payment." When his father heard that, he hit the roof and said the wedding gowns for the wives of all three of Kent's brothers didn't cost $2,500 altogether. Kent also indicated his dad was growing nervous about the amount of money he was spending on Mechele's house in Wasilla and other things.

The Leppink family was expecting Mechele to come to Florida while Kent was there, but when she didn't show up (Mechele was traveling with Hilke), he scrambled to cover for her. "Since we couldn't get together to talk about our wedding with my family," he wrote on April 7, "I was the only one around to talk for you. Or, should I use some other word?

All week long I got questions about you and when you'd be coming. I had to make a lot of excuses. Needless to say, I think it is best if you hold off on ordering the dress right now. If you really want to know why, get in touch with me. We have six months to go until we get married. We need to spend the first few days of that six months talking."

Kent came home the next night, April 8, a little more than three weeks before his murder, and sent a fast note to Mechele, who was still traveling. His note included this citation from the Bible, given to him by his father.

> "Love is patient and kind,
> it doesn't envy or boast
> and it's never proud.
> It's not rude or selfish,
> It doesn't get angry easily
> Or keep track of wrongs.
> Love doesn't delight in bad things,
> But it rejoices in the truth.
> Love always protects,
> Trusts, hopes, and perseveres.
> Love never fails."

Getting the Bible passage instead of a check set Mechele to smoldering, though she responded only with this low-key but pointed email,

"Sorry, the dress is already ordered and paid for. You should have told me that two weeks ago when I asked about it. I don't want to discuss it while I am this upset."

Kent answered, "Two weeks ago I asked you about the dress and the cost. I didn't get an answer and then in Florida the shit hit the fan between my parents and me. If there is no way to do anything else about the dress but to get it, we will find some way to pay for it. I want to be part of the plans from now on, not to infringe upon your wishes, but to keep them within our means.

"Yes it is your dress," he wrote, "and I won't be seeing you in it until you walk down the aisle. I need to know about it now, though. What is it going to cost? I don't want to know what it looks like. You wouldn't get anything that wasn't beautiful. I want to know what I am going to have to do in order to get this dress for you. Now please tell me what the total cost of the dress is going to be and if you think that we can afford it. Is it possible to get something less expensive yet still be OK for you? Let's do the planning from now on together."

She responded with a short note saying it was too late to change plans since the wedding dress had already been ordered and the bill paid—though what actually happened may have been Mechele's using borrowed money to pay the premium for the insurance on Kent's life. The wedding dress was never presented as evidence and may never have existed.

CHAPTER 23
'Let's Just Elope'

Carlin became angry when Hilke sent him a message saying Mechele had told him about Carlin's having a fling with a male prostitute. The former steel man concealed his resentment in a chatty email to her on a variety of subjects. But near the end he added the comment, "You really enjoy telling people that I was with a whore that was a man, don't you?"

Carlin apparently left his computer and returned to find that Kent had been looking through his messages again. "I just noticed that Kent went through all my letters on the computer when I was gone," he wrote to Mechele. "He does a bad job of covering his tracks now that I know what to look for."

Kent apparently didn't realize that he could have used the email application to mark the missives as unread, which would have made his snooping difficult to detect. But, he might also have wanted Carlin and Mechele to know he was looking over their shoulders. Given his "Gotcha" surprises of previous months, either is a real possibility.

The next day, Kent received an email from his brother Craig, apparently warning him against marrying too hastily.

"You don't have to worry about me rushing into something," Kent replied. "We have been engaged for one-and-a-half years now. Seems much too long to me, but every day we learn more about each other. Good times, and bad times, but we continue to grow together. All I can hope for is the best. Our age difference is sometimes a problem, but as time goes by, even that gap gets narrower. She makes me younger, and I mature her a little. (I much prefer a younger woman to an older one .... don't you think?) Actually, we don't think of ourselves in terms of being older or younger than one another. In many things, she is more mature than I am, and vice versa. We really complement each other well."

On April 9 he sent her an apologetic note. The tone indicated that she had called the night before, they argued, and she hung up on him. He wrote that the argument was entirely his fault, and that he had been misleading her by spending so much money on her, giving her a false impression that he was wealthy.

"Spending every dime I had and then asking my dad for more only put up a false front to you. It made you feel you had an unlimited budget by which you could just go out and do anything you wanted to. I wish I could do this for you, but at this time, I am not able to do it. I know that I have given you that impression and I am sorry for it. It makes me feel as if I have been buying your love."

She responded with a curt note telling him to stop worrying about the money for the insurance policies because her grandfather had made her a gift of the cash. She then asked if he had gone by the New York Life office and signed the policies. She said her grandfather expected to get a copy of the policies and was getting peeved because the envelope hadn't come.

"He hasn't gotten anything and is wondering what I have done with that $. I am losing his trust and I don't like it," she wrote. Mechele said she thought Carlin might buy the land in Costa Rica for the bird sanctuary, which would allow them to make a profit on operating it, and they might also be able to buy Carlin's house for a low price when he went back to New Jersey.

Kent answered that he had signed the insurance policies and had the copies there at the house.

In an email on April 20, eleven days before his murder, Kent told Mechele once again of his intense love for her. He described being out fishing, "People must have thought strange thoughts of me because I had a smile on my face," he wrote. "I had a dream about you, and you were walking down the aisle in the most beautiful wedding gown ever made. Only you were more beautiful. I can't wait until our wedding day. You are going to be the most beautiful bride ever, and we are going to have a wonderful wedding. I love you so much and only want the best for you."

The very next day she wrote back, furious again at his compulsive snooping and threatened to call off the wedding. She said from then on she would change the way they end their arguments. Complaining that he whines and answers questions evasively, she said, "Rather than get frustrated with you, I am going to walk away and stop the argument and my frustration, so if you do this you know what to expect. When you want to try again, we can until you stop snooping, which you are still doing as of last Friday. You and I will not get married and will not have a life. This is not a request any more. This is a threat. The first time was a warning and a request. Three strikes, Kent, you are out and stay out. I won't have it in my life.

"[N]ot just the snooping, the continued evasiveness, trying not to give me straight info. I ask for simple answers ... not as complicated as the shit you say. I am wearing thin of this, and the other night when we were fighting and I asked you why you were whining and you said you were making fun of me, well, fuck you. You really hurt me by saying that. I do not whine and you have since the day I met you, so blame that one on your mother, not me."

The email also contained wording suggesting that John Carlin might consider himself dying, perhaps from the lead poisoning for which he received the settlement money for exposure to lead-based paint. She said Carlin had made her the beneficiary of his insurance, with the understanding that she would care for his son. The references could simply relate to the fact that Carlin planned to return to New Jersey and resume his life as a steelworker, but the words seemed more ominous than that.

"John does not know about his father," she wrote. "He just lost his mother and it would be hard on him for big John to tell him. John has made me his beneficiary to his insurance policy with instructions on what to do. As you can see, little John will be part of my life (and hopefully your) life for a while. I gave him my word and must do this for him."

Mechele said she planned to ask Carlin to leave his son with her when he moved east. "John is 17 and will be going on his own soon, and I just want him to develop a relationship with me so when it happens, he can come to me."

Mechele then suggested that she and Kent forget about an elaborate wedding and simply elope. "I think if you still want to marry me, we should just go and do it. We don't need our families there. We just need each other and some trust between us. We don't need a big wedding or guests or the expense that goes with it. We should get married within the next month. We should just do it and start our life. We need nothing else. Love always from Me"

For investigators, prosecutors and court juries, the big problem with much of the evidence collected from Mechele's laptop and Carlin's desktop computer is that there are two possible explanations for even the most suspicious pieces—

one guilty and one innocent.

A classic example can be found in a long email from Carlin to Mechele on April 24, a week before the murder. His note was in answer to an emotional one from her. Mechele's email was apparently not found by investigators, but Carlin responds by trying to comfort her and quotes from it extensively. Though she is preparing for a tryst with Scott Hilke, Carlin's email suggests Mechele might be emotionally torn at the prospect of Carlin's pending departure.

"You wrote that 'I feel like part of me is leaving, like I can't stop it ... I am so scared that you will never be in my life again and I don't think that's what I want.'"

Carlin replied, "I am assuming that the 'part of you is leaving' is a reference to me. I am also assuming that the 'I am so scared that you will never be in my life again' is a reference to me leaving the state of Alaska and throwing in the towel." He added that he was flattered and pleased that she was so concerned about losing him, but was giving up because he knew he would never win the competition for her heart.

"I am and have been here for you, waiting and hoping," he wrote. "I think you would feel the same way if I was going to an old or present girlfriend every opportunity that I had. You would think that I was less than sincere when telling you how important you are to me as I pack my clothes to fly off to see another.

"In a letter I wrote to you, I said I felt like a second-string player hanging around to see if the first-string player fails. You didn't like that and said it is not true. You say, 'hang in there, Scott will mess up'. I hate to tell you this, but that is what a second-string player is. Someone who sticks around in case the primary player fails. I am the second choice, at least right now.

"You said, 'If only I knew what I wanted, I would not hurt

so many people. I would not mess with others' lives'. This is normal for people such as us. It is nothing to worry about. Your happiness and needs (outweigh) the needs and happiness of me or others. And I want it that way; your happiness and needs coming first. I think you know what you want and would have to settle for second best with me. I have tried my best and it was just not good enough."

Carlin also included a few words that suggest another source for Mechele's angst. He had told her he could no longer afford to support her while she was dating Hilke. "Its not that I do not want to," he wrote. "I just cannot afford to support you while you do this. I cannot financially afford to put thousands of dollars into Scott's home, pay for your tickets to go see him, and give you spending money to have fun with him while you are there. I don't have the money to do that. I wish that I did. Things would probably be different if I had the money. I would keep you happy by traveling all over having fun with you and you would forget Scott. I just don't have the money. I am sorry for that. Please forgive me."

Carlin also mentioned a term she had used in reference to him, one from her strip club days. He said she had referred to him as "a mark I got too close to."

"I knew this from the beginning," he said. "I just wanted to be your friend and I was the one that got close to you ... correction, fell so deeply in love with you that I threw away my common sense and went for happiness. You were not being selfish, just being Mechele, the most beautiful person in the world. The one I have fallen in love with. The one I would do anything in the world for, including giving up my life. I just love you so much."

The long and emotional message also included a few words that could mean anything from a murder plot to assurance that she will get along quite well with him [Carlin] gone back East.

"You will be just fine Mechele. Just give it a few weeks. Your life is about to get a lot better. You will see."

On April 27, four days before the murder, while Mechele was at Lake Tahoe with Hilke, she wrote a furious all-caps letter to Carlin. She was angry at Kent again because of his complaints about her mishandling of the laptop computer and his snooping.

"HE IS SUCH A SHIT; HE SENT ME A LETTER ASKING WHERE THE COMP IS. SAID I MAY HAVE DAMAGED IT THE WAY I UNPLUGGED IT. IT SHOULD BE EASIER THAN THIS. I HOPE HE SHOWS UP BEFORE HIS DAD. WHERE IS HIS DIDDY BAG? I THINK HE WILL COME HOME TO CHANGE CLOTHES. BUT IT'S STILL LIGHT OUT AT THAT TIME, SO MAYBE HE WON'T ... SEE YOU SOON. SORRY YOU HAD THAT FEELING AT THE AIRPORT. I KNOW WHAT IT IS. I HATE IT. TT PROB. HAS ALREADY SPOTTED MY CAR AT THE AIRPORT. LOVE YOU. CALL THIS EVENING."

CHAPTER 24
The Witnesses

The sizable file of emails and partial emails recovered from the two computers added a puzzling aspect to the case. In the context of a known murder, they could be considered evidence of a growing plot to kill a man who annoyed and sometimes infuriated his housemates. But, without that murder, they would simply be volleys of messages between people in an emotionally wrenching situation that might or might not have led to violence. By themselves, they could not prove either that a murder took place or that Mechele and John Carlin were planning such a murder. The fact that Kent was shot to death did not make irrefutable evidence, but it did cause both jurors and spectators to suspect that one led to the other.

Judge Volland walked a fine line on the question of young Carlin as an alternate suspect in his father's case. Early in the trial, the only information before the court suggesting the boy's possible guilt was a reference to him as a suspect in a search warrant. At that time Volland ruled that young Carlin could not be argued as a likely suspect.

Later, when legal motions were being considered prior to closing arguments, he reversed himself. By that time, Volland and the jurors had heard testimony suggesting that the possibility did indeed exist that the boy was the killer. " … that's probably how jurors are perceiving John Carlin IV anyway at this point," Volland noted. "So I'll permit specific reference to him during closing."

Though only John Carlin III was being tried—and Mechele Linehan's trial was yet to come—Mechele was virtually tried in absentia by the remarks of both Carlin's defense lawyers and the prosecution. After frequent comments about Mechele during the course of the proceedings, prosecutor Gullufsen noted in the opening of his summation, "One of the first obsessions ... that dominates here is Mechele Hughes wants money. She was obsessed by it. She has a drive to get it, and she had no moral qualms about how to get it."

Only then did he get to the actual defendant in that trial. "John Carlin had an obsession that almost matched Mechele's," Gullufsen said. "It was different, though. It was an obsession for her, and he would do anything to make her happy, including giving up his life."

The prosecution's claim of obsession—as it had throughout the trial— added to the lurid quality of the news coverage and gave reporters in the jammed courtroom more fodder for readers already enthralled by the tale of a beautiful ex-stripper turned soccer mom; the term was used frequently, though Mechele's daughter was not a soccer player.

Gullufsen quoted from an undated email written by Carlin to Mechele and retrieved from one of the computers. "I want to reiterate that I will never leave you, cheat on you, desire anyone but you, and I will worship the ground you walk on, the air you breathe, the words you speak, and the glow of your being. I will love you forever."

In recounting the lavish material gifts Carlin had given her and the thousands he spent on her, he mentioned the million-dollar life insurance policy. "Kent Leppink was worth a lot of money to Mechele," Gullufsen said. "And she can get the money all at once in a huge, lump sum, but there's one condition: Kent has to die ... Kent's death is what Mechele wants. She engineered the whole life insurance scenario ... and John was willing to make it happen."

Gullufsen said the timing of Kent's murder was forced on the plotters by Kent's plans to leave for the season on his fishing tender and his irrational obsession with Mechele. Kent had convinced himself that Mechele was going to marry him, and he was pushing to make sure it happened soon.

"Kent is not going to go away quietly," Gullufsen said. "Let's put it that way. He's got his family involved in this marriage; he's got his whole ego and being involved in this marriage. He's obsessed with it. He's not going to walk away, and they know that.

"Ms. Hughes' day of reckoning is coming, because I will be prosecuting her, and we will be putting on a case against her, and we have charged her with murder in the first degree as an accomplice or principal in Kent Leppink's death. But now is the time for his reckoning. Now is the time to come back under this evidence with a guilty verdict against John Carlin, and I and a different jury and defense counsel will then deal with Mechele Hughes. Thank you."

The jury deliberated for two days, then returned on April 3, 2007, with a verdict of "guilty of murder in the first degree as charged in the indictment." Carlin's legal team asked that sentencing be delayed until after Mechele's trial in the fall of 2007. The prosecutor agreed and Judge Volland set sentencing for the following November 9.

As the verdict was read, Kent Leppink's father sat weeping in the audience. After the jury ruled Carlin guilty, defense lawyer Marcy McDannel told a reporter, "What this means is the real bad player in all of this, the real evil participant in all of this, has a chance of getting off."

CHAPTER 25
Her Trial

Mechele went on trial before Judge Volland in September, 2007. Representing her were lawyers Kevin T. Fitzgerald of Anchorage and Wayne C. Fricke of Tacoma. The prosecutor was again Gullufsen of the state Attorney General's office.

Mechele went into the trial with at least three strikes against her, more than even the average defendant. The most obvious was her past job as a stripper, a profession carrying with it the implication—deserved or not—that dancers are sinners inhabiting the outer fringes of the underworld.[9]

Another strike was the fact that she was an attractive and apparently manipulative woman, which proved to be a cause for suspicion with many of the 11 women on the jury. The third was the same problem all defendants face, the fact that police believed she was guilty, believed it strongly enough to arrest her. After all, the thinking goes, she wouldn't be on trial if there weren't good reason to believe she did it.

The assumption of guilt—universally made by the news media, the public, and even juries—flies in the face of the American legal principle that you are considered innocent until

---

[9] In fact, many dancers are merely working women, some married and living as housewives during the day, who accept the work as a way to earn a lot of money legally in a fairly short period of time.

Dead Man's Dancer

proven guilty. It is nonetheless a fact of life in the courtroom.[10]

It probably did not help Mechele's cause that Judge Volland had also presided over Carlin's trial and was exposed to a large volume of testimony and legal argument blaming her for the murder. She was, in fact, used as a scapegoat in the Carlin trial, somebody to blame who wasn't on trial at the moment. While Volland is a respected and professional jurist, it's difficult to believe that he could listen to the evidence considered in the Carlin trial and hear frequent accusations by witnesses and by Carlin's lawyers without being influenced by what he heard.

Mechele's guilt or innocence would be decided by a jury, so asking for a different judge would be difficult to justify, but the built-in anomalies of the judicial system meant Volland would sit through both trials and do his best to remain unbiased. Volland's rulings in her case were not likely to be influenced by what he had heard in Carlin's earlier trial, but the persistent anti-Mechele argument and testimony in the first proceedings created an unpromising atmosphere for her trial.[11]

The jury selection for Mechele's trial was also an odd affair. Fitzgerald, the lead defense attorney, was convinced that male jurors would be more sympathetic to Mechele's plight than would women, who might be put off by the three strikes described above. But, the prospective male jurors called for questioning before being seated—when asked how they felt about the credibility of exotic dancers (as Fitzgerald preferred to have them called)—almost always responded with a variation of the answer, "You can't trust those dancers."

Fitzgerald had been a prosecutor and a criminal defense lawyer since 1995, handling murder cases, gangbanger

---

10 Wyoming lawyer Gerry Spence, one of the nation's leading defense attorneys, explains the reality of courtroom guilt assumption in his book, "The Smoking Gun."

11 An example of the harsh statements made about Mechele in the John Carlin trial had come when lawyer Sidney Billingslea said of her, "She's a lying, scheming, manipulative person." Since Mechele was not on trial at the time, there was no one to refute the accusation.

defenses, and all manner of criminal cases. He was not naive. But he grew up in an Anchorage where stories were still told about the years before World War II, when the whorehouse madam was likely to be the justice of the peace in her spare time. The heyday of the bawdyhouses was long past, but until he began interviewing prospective male jurors for Mechele Linehan's trial, he had no idea just how much the city's culture had changed.

Fitzgerald assumed that men between 20 and 30 would understand when an attractive woman took her clothes off to entertain a mostly male audience. The houses had moved out of the downtown area but surely, he thought, single men would sympathize with the women who danced for lonely men. This generation seemed almost prudish.

Fitzgerald was also shocked by the response of one prospective female juror who admitted she sometimes danced at The Bush Company on amateur night. Surely she would be sympathetic, but the woman gave essentially the same answer offered by many of the men, "You can't trust those dancers."

In the end the defense lawyer had to deal with a jury panel composed of 12 women and two men. After two were dismissed as the trial entered the deliberations phase, the jury consisted of 11 women and one man, an unpromising group to decide the fate of the ex-stripper who married a doctor.

During the trial, Fitzgerald called a nationally known forensic psychiatrist to testify on Mechele's behalf. Dr. Mark Mills reported that he tested her while she was in prison awaiting trial and found it was very unlikely that Mechele had committed or instigated the murder. Mills said that if she was responsible, the tests would have shown one pattern of responses. If she had been involved but later had a guilt-induced epiphany that enabled her to become a virtuous doctor's wife living in the suburbs, the tests would have shown another distinctive pattern. What they did show, he said, was a person who was not likely involved in the murder at all but was somewhat naive and overwhelmed by her circumstances.

The psychiatrist's testimony was largely ignored after it came out that he had administered the primary test, the Minnesota Multiphasic Personality Inventory, when he arrived at the Hiland Mountain Correctional Facility after a long flight to Anchorage. He decided to save time and get back to his hotel room, so he gave the test to Mechele and asked her to fill it out in her room. He would pick it up in the morning.

Since the jury couldn't tell whether the questions had been answered by Mechele or a roommate, or by Mechele in collaboration with other prisoners, the test results were given virtually no credence and didn't come up for discussion again in the trial until Judge Volland reviewed and dismissed them. An Anchorage psychoanalyst who studied the psychiatrist's findings suggested to this author that the Linehan family should ask for their money back on the consulting fee paid for the man's services.

When John Carlin IV testified at Mechele Linehan's trial in October, he winked at Mechele as he walked to the witness stand. After testifying, young Carlin walked away from the stand smiling. When asked outside the courtroom what he meant by the wink, young Carlin said he wanted to reassure Mechele. "She's like a sister to me," he said.

From the stand, young Carlin told much the same story he had given at his father's trial a few months previous, but this time embellished it even further. He said he saw his father and Mechele washing the pistol with bleach hours after he had picked up the gun from a hallway floor. He said he believed his father washed the pistol to get rid of fingerprints left from the son's handling of the gun.

Young Carlin's sometimes odd behavior also involved an

obscene gesture to a television photographer at the courtroom's entrance during Mechele's trial and an incident calling another photographer for the same station a "fag." A photo of Carlin's furious face behind his raised middle finger was published on the station's Website with the headline, "Boy behaving badly." The station discreetly blocked the image of young Carlin's finger.

Mechele's trial was further enlivened by testimony from a former Bush Company dancer who said she and Mechele saw the movie *The Last Seduction* together and Mechele had told her she wanted to be just like the charismatic woman in the film. *The Last Seduction*, starring Linda Fiorentino, is about a woman who manipulates her lover into killing her husband for $700,000 in drug money, then walks away rich when the lover is arrested.

But that testimony was undermined when the second dancer, Lora Aspiotis, by then a 43-year-old stay-at-home mother in South Carolina, was ordered to produce her personal diaries for the period. When she delivered the diaries, they showed Aspiotis saw the film with her own husband and not with Mechele, though that still left open the possibility that Mechele had made such a remark to Aspiotis. But the woman's obviously imperfect memory compromised her testimony, suggesting that she may have retrofitted her memory of seeing the movie with Mechele to conform to events after the Alaska murder.

Prosecutor Gullufsen tried to have the film entered as evidence in the case, but Judge Volland ruled that it was too unlike the Linehan case and the jury would not be allowed to see it. Gullufsen did manage to reference the film and its thriller plot in his presentation, including his dramatic closing arguments.

Gullufsen noted in his comments that email recovered from the two computers indicated Mechele and Carlin were almost totally focused on Kent in the last five days of April, 1996. Of the 13 email messages found by the forensic experts during those five days, 11 of them were from Mechele to Carlin and ten of those were about Kent. In the last few days there were also 12 or 13 telephone calls from the condo she was sharing with Hilke in Tahoe to the house in South Anchorage, a total of approximately two hours of conversation.[12]

Gullufsen said the pace of both email and telephone traffic far exceeded that of her previous trips, an indication that Mechele had a sense of urgency this time. And since a jury had already found Carlin guilty of murdering Kent Leppink, Gullufsen could and did argue that the urgency was motivated by their plans for the murder and the approaching time. In further support for the Mechele Linehan as murder conspirator argument, Gullufsen noted that, when the shooting occurred, she had only recently paid the premium on the million-dollar life insurance policy and likely did not know that she was no longer the beneficiary. He noted that she rarely paid for anything herself, relying instead on others to pay her bills. But the insurance premium was a notable exception.

Gullufsen said Mechele called the New York Life office from Tahoe and asked if the policy could be canceled and the premium refunded, but he said Mechele knew it could only be done in person, not by telephone. The purpose of the call, the prosecutor argued, was to find out if Kent had canceled the policy. He said she then assumed, from the vague answer she got from the insurance agent's assistant, that the policy was still in force and she was the primary beneficiary.

Gullufsen argued, "At the same time that she is telling Kent how much she loves him and how she wants to marry him and setting up dates, at the same time she is writing email to

---

12 Detective Stogsdill speculated in an interview that she was trying to "jack up" Carlin and get him to carry out the murder before she returned from Tahoe.

John Carlin about how she can't live without him, how he is so important to her, that he is the reason she exists, and what we have going on here basically, is these two fellows are being set up for her ulterior goal—to collect on the insurance policy and use one of them to kill the other, and John Carlin makes it very clear in those emails that he'll pretty much do, too, what Mechele ends up asking him."

Gullufsen's argument dismisses the fact that Carlin has declared in an email that he is giving up the competition for Mechele's heart and going back to New Jersey. The prosecutor cited another email in which Mechele told Carlin, "I love you very much, I miss you, I can't wait to go on our getaway. Did you know that you can buy a citizenship in the Seychelles for around 10 mil and no matter what crimes you have committed they will not extradite? They are the only country that won't send you back to the U.S."

When Scott Hilke was called to the witness stand during Mechele's trial, he was upset and hostile toward her, apparently because he had been dragged into the case as a possible suspect. Hilke also raised the possibility—perhaps inadvertently—that young John Carlin was present at the murder scene when Kent was killed. In response to questions, he told the court about his call to Anchorage on May 3 from his California home. He said he called to make sure Mechele got home safely after her trip to Lake Tahoe with him. Hilke testified that young John Carlin answered his call and told him Kent had been killed. He said the boy told him Kent had been "gut-shot."

Mechele and the Carlins had only been notified of Kent's murder earlier that day. Massie and Brandenburger, the two officers who gave them the news and interviewed them, had been deliberately vague about the details of Kent's wounds. Giving a graphic description of the victim's injuries would have been a serious violation of normal police procedure.[13]

It's possible, though seems unlikely, that young John's father (or even Mechele) could have told the boy about the stomach wound. Carlin's sharing of that information—if he had it—seems doubtful, and so does the possibility that Mechele told him. Such a statement would have been an admission of direct knowledge of the murder. A "slip of the lip" in such circumstances is similarly unlikely. The personalities of the two suggest they were more likely to be reticent and unwilling to talk about such details, if they had them.

Later in Mechele's trial, her Tacoma lawyer Wayne Fricke pointed out that the boy also told differing stories about the washing of the pistol after the murder. In 2005—when the Alaska Cold Case detectives interviewed him—and in 2006—when a Seattle police detective questioned him—he said Mechele was not present when his father was washing the gun with bleach. He said she may have been elsewhere in the house. Yet when he testified before an Alaska grand jury later in 2006, young Carlin said Mechele was standing in the bathroom door while his father washed fingerprints from the big .44 in the sink. That statement before the grand jury was made after he had been told by investigator Linda Branchflower that he was a suspect in the case.

Despite her email to Kent suggesting a loving, if troubled, relationship, Mechele told detectives and network television interviewers that she and Kent only pretended to be engaged because he was actually homosexual. The pretense was for the benefit of his parents, she said; he didn't want them to know about his real sexual orientation.[14]

---

13 How young Carlin could have known that Kent Leppink was shot in the stomach, among other places, is an interesting question. The two officers who met with Mechele and Carlin that day did not tell them anything about Kent's wounds. In fact, Trooper Massie, now retired, says he and his partner, Trooper Brandenburger, had not been briefed on the coroner's report at that point and didn't have the information about the stomach wound.

14 In an interview with Anchorage Daily News reporter Megan Holland, the elder Carlin said he

Though Kent did have at least one homosexual affair and his feigned sex with young John Carlin could have been a crude attempt at humor, his affection and intensity for Mechele seems indisputable. Detectives believed the email note contradicted her claim that the engagement was only a pretense and they never intended to marry. In one note on April 5, Mechele was getting testy about Kent's failure to send her a check for $2,500 for the wedding gown and veil. She indicated she had already paid for them by borrowing the money from her grandfather, and now needed to pay Granddad back.

The movie *The Last Seduction* also became a problem for Mechele in her trial despite the fact that Judge Volland ruled that it could not be used as evidence and refused to allow the jury to see it. Gullufsen continued to use its plot to influence the jurors. He reminded the jury that both dancer Lora Aspiotis and Scott Hilke had said it was one of Mechele's favorite movies. The movie and its plot were relatively well known at the time and some news coverage of the arrests and indictments included the apparent similarity of the plot to the case.

"You know, John Carlin pulled the trigger and he's going to pay for it," Gullufsen said, "and we all agree that he's guilty and he ought to, but he had a partner. He had someone who really set this up neatly. He had someone who promoted it, facilitated it, and aided and abetted him in doing it, and that's Mechele Hughes, Mechele Linehan. Now, if she's going to write the script, if she's the one who's going to write the ending to this, it's going to be just like the movie, isn't it. Problem is, you're going to write the ending, she isn't; and it's not going to be a false and contrived ending, one that she would have. It's

---

thought Kent was troubled about his sexuality. He said the fisherman was "a homosexual that was very unhappy with being a homosexual. He portrayed very openly a macho-man imagery. But he was very effeminate.... I remember once when Avon man come to the door, he actually ran around Mechele who was walking to the door to get it, and he got two of everything. He sat there and he put lotion on his feet, lotion on his head."

Dead Man's Dancer 117

going to be a true and it's going to be a just ending, because the proof is beyond a reasonable doubt that she aided and abetted and solicited the murder of Kent Leppink, and it's time to hold her accountable for that. Thank you."

Kevin Fitzgerald noted in his summation for the defense that the volume of telephone calls and email between Mechele and Carlin—and sometimes Kent—was not unusual for that household. He said the rush to get the insurance policy signed and effective was because the fishing season was about to get started. Kent and Mechele were buying a new tender boat through their M&K business, and the time when insurance was needed on Kent's life, because of the boat liability, was fast approaching.

Fitzgerald conceded that Mechele had behaved badly in many ways, an apparent reference to both her treatment of her lovers and the comment to her sister that Kent deserved to die and should have been tortured. But at that time she was under tremendous pressure, especially since Kent had named her in his list of people who might kill him— an accusation to which police would lend great credence. She was emotionally torn after the murder. "All this kind of mudslinging at Mrs. Linehan shows immaturity in relationships, shows confusion in the relationships, shows lack of honesty in the relationships, demonstrates she said some lousy things, but you know what? She's not charged with any of those things."

He said evidence that she had been a girl behaving badly did not prove that she solicited the murder of Kent Leppink. It showed instead that Mechele and Carlin were drifting apart, that Carlin was upset both by Kent's presence in the house— and the dampening effect that had on Carlin's own prospects for winning Mechele—and Kent's feigning of anal sex with John's son. Fitzgerald cited the elder Carlin's apparent homophobia and self-disgust because of his own bisexual adventures.

Fitzgerald said the evidence showed that the Hope note was written to make Kent think Mechele was in Hope rather than in Tahoe. And when Mechele worried that Kent might find her car and realize she was actually traveling via airline, she sent an email suggesting that Carlin tell Kent that she had flown to Barrow to see Reddell. That would have undermined the credibility of the Hope note, but it would help head off the possibility of an embarrassing confrontation in Tahoe, a more urgent consideration.

"Ladies and gentlemen," he added, "what we ask is that you return Mrs. Linehan to Olympia. We ask that you return her to her family and to her friends and to her husband and to her daughter, and we ask that you return the only true and just verdict in this case, which is to find that Mrs. Linehan is not guilty."

The jurors returned their verdict on Oct. 22, 2007. They decided that Mechele was "guilty." The verdict stunned many observers who suspected Mechele might have played a role in the death of Kent Leppink, but didn't think the prosecutor had proved it was the cold-blooded plot described by the news media.

As the jury verdict was read, Mechele stood beside her husband and Fitzgerald. When she heard the word guilty, she slumped to her seat. Her husband knelt beside her and buried his head in her shoulder. When guards stepped forward to handcuff her, Mechele embraced Colin one final time before they led her away.

Among the most shocked by the verdict was Kevin Fitzgerald, who had waited while the jury deliberated, convinced that he had won the case and that the evidence was just not substantive enough to send his client to prison. He was sure the jury would find Mechele not guilty of at least the worst charges against her. Many in the Alaska community, which followed the case as it unfolded in the media each day, had made the same assumption. Fitzgerald's shock was widely shared.

CHAPTER 26
Two in Prison

Outside the courthouse after the verdict, juror Christine Eagleson told reporter Megan Holland that she and her fellow jurors were convinced of Mechele's guilt by the emails. "If you take one of those emails alone," she said, "then it doesn't have the same impact it does when you stack them up like you would stack bricks. And, I think when that happened, you ended up building something really large and, I think, undeniable."[15]

The juror also admitted that Mechele's former life as a stripper helped convince them that she was capable of the crime. "When you were soliciting yourself to be attractive sexually in all those ways," she told the reporter, "you were soliciting yourself in that manner for money—that all goes into the factor of manipulation and seduction. That was a whole key point that we discussed on and on and on."

Holland then called Carlin at the Anchorage Jail, where he was awaiting sentencing for his own conviction. Carlin had seen a television news flash about the Linehan verdict and told

---

[15] Author's Note — The emails were indeed the bricks of the case and reading them one after the other does create great suspicion, but the letter from the grave was the mortar binding the bricks together. Mechele's profession as a stripper, her lifestyle and her treatment of lovers gave a strong impression of a manipulator, but without the mortar of the high-impact letter and its pointing finger, the wall and the case seem to fall apart.

Dead Man's Dancer

Holland that Linehan's defense lawyers had "shot themselves in the foot by not presenting the truth of what happened. The truth gets muddled when both sides are making things up." Carlin told the reporter, "There's nothing in any one of those emails that has anything about his (Kent's) death." Carlin reiterated his previous claim that the note about the cabin in Hope was nothing more than a device to prevent Kent from finding Mechele in California.

While at Spring Creek Prison in Seward, still awaiting sentencing, Carlin told an interviewer from the CBS Sixty Minutes program that he lied about not owning the Desert Eagle because he was under "intense scrutiny." He conceded it was probably the murder weapon but said it disappeared from his house around the time Kent Leppink was murdered.

Carlin told CBS that when the gun fell out of the hall closet at his son's feet, "I heard Mechele yelling 'don't touch it … don't touch it!'" He said he rounded the hall corner and came face-to-face with a glaring Mechele. That was when he became worried about his son's fingerprints being on the gun and cleaned it in a bleach solution in the bathroom sink.

CHAPTER 27
99 Years

In sentencing John Carlin, Judge Volland noted that Carlin had been free for ten years after the murder and kept Kent Leppink's deer statue on display in his living room as something of a trophy. He said, "Mr. Carlin is a worst offender just on the basis of the nature of the act, and that is an intentional, premeditated homicide." The judge said the jury's verdict established that "it was Mr. Carlin who lured Kent Leppink to Hope, that it was Mr. Carlin who pulled the trigger, and the last time he did it, most likely, was looking a dying Kent Leppink straight in the eyes ... this was truly murder with malice aforethought.

"It was committed against a friend and a housemate. It was done for the most venal of reasons, and it was a killing that was cold and it was calculated and it was cruel. Because of that, I believe that a maximum sentence is warranted."

Volland sentenced Carlin to serve 99 years in prison, a term that would make him eligible for parole in 33 years, when he would be age 82.

In Mechele's sentencing hearing, numerous witnesses testified to her life as a loving mother and good neighbor. They described her as a person who would risk her own life to help another. Considering the way she lived, the way she treated other people as well as birds and animals, she could not be the evil person described by the prosecution and investigators. One of her friends from her dancing days said Mechele behaved like that even in 1994, long before Kent's murder and before she left Alaska.

Prosecutor Gullufsen said in his sentencing statement that Mechele was able to do such good things because she had destroyed evidence and covered up her crime. She was able to live free for ten years because she succeeded in avoiding prosecution. "Given the things she did to avoid prosecution, to get rid of evidence, to twist the circumstances to mislead the investigators," Gullufsen said, "she shouldn't get credit for a good life that she only had an opportunity to accomplish because she did underlying bad things, which is cover up a murder."

Defense lawyer Kevin Fitzgerald said in his own sentencing statement that he was shocked by the verdict. He said he talked to some of the jurors and was unsatisfied with their explanation of why they found Mechele Linehan guilty. He said it appeared to be based on a feeling—provoked by the ambiguous emails—that convinced them of her guilt.

Fitzgerald said the media frenzy surrounding the case had created a toxic environment that made a fair trial difficult. The problem included coverage of John Carlin's trial a few months earlier and the emphasis on Mechele and the finger-pointing in the Carlin trial. During those proceedings, "The Alaskan media focused a sensationalized spotlight on Mechele Linehan to such an extent that one would have thought it was she on trial rather than Mr. Carlin ... the steady diet of scandalous Mechele Linehan stories many weeks before she stood trial, together with the ... incessant tabloidesque media treatment of her trial, seriously compromised Mechele Linehan's opportunity to receive a fair trial in Alaska."

As she had during much of the trial, Mechele listened to the legal arguments wearing a government-issued jumpsuit with her hair tied in a ponytail. Though routinely described as attractive in news accounts of her dancing career, Mechele looked more like a forlorn prisoner in her courtroom appearances.

Among those who were not convinced of Mechele's guilt was Julie Thrasher, one of the alternate jurors who was dismissed at the close of testimony to bring the panel down to 12 members. Thrasher sent a letter to Judge Volland saying she was convinced that Mechele did not participate in the murder of Kent Leppink and should be acquitted.

Thrasher said far too many pieces of evidence could be interpreted one way or another. "Every piece of evidence offered could be looked at with a different spin on it," she wrote. "There's too much 'could be this, but could be that,' attached to the evidence in this case.

"If I had been able to deliberate in this case, maybe, just maybe there would have been a not guilty verdict. However, without doubt you would have had a hung jury because, as I stated, the evidence did not prove her guilt beyond a reasonable doubt. I would have stood by my understanding of the evidence, not how she supported herself—the evidence."

Thrasher asked for lenience for Mechele and said she felt "Mrs. Linehan should be free and with her family this day instead of awaiting sentencing due to a guilty verdict that in my opinion was decided for all the wrong reasons."

Another unnamed juror, one who had remained on the panel through the verdict and was convinced that Mechele was involved in the murder plot, sent a letter asking for the lightest sentence possible. "Mechele is a good person, not a threat to society. She did get her education, have a daughter and strived and worked hard with her husband to give her daughter something she never had.

"The men she was involved with knew exactly what they were doing. They were adults ... there simply isn't anything in this record which would suggest that isolation is a paramount concern, that the public needs her to be isolated in order to protect them, that any person or persons needs that. In fact, the opposite is true.

"The opposite, Judge, demonstrates that her community needs her, her friends need her, her husband and her daughter need her, and for that I request that you impose the least sentence minimally possible."

Then it was Mechele's turn to be heard. Though she had never testified or spoken publicly during the trial, she gave an emotionally powerful statement which she read aloud to Judge Volland and the jammed courtroom gallery.

"Your Honor," she said, "I'd like to introduce myself to you. I've sat here in your courtroom and never had a chance to tell you about myself. I am not the monster that has been painted by the prosecution. I have not lived a life of greed ... or that of this fictional character of a Hollywood movie that has been portrayed by the prosecution. I am 35, I'm a wife to a wonderful man who I love dearly, I'm a mother to a bright-eyed little girl who is and always will be the brightest star in my life.

"I'm a business owner. I work overtime every week. My husband and I and my daughter, we have a simple life. We live in a home that was built in 1904. We drive old vehicles. We spend our weekends and evenings at home repairing and restoring our home, gardening and cooking. We enjoy skiing and running, cycling and camping and watch Star Wars movies together. Our home is always bellowing with life.

"The weekends and holidays are always filled with people. The kids make their own pizzas, carve pumpkins and ice Christmas cookies. The adults flow through the rooms, have conversations by a quiet fireplace. Our life has never been decadent or extravagant or lavish. I'm telling you this so that you can have a visualization of how we live our life from me.

"Our home is simple. Our life is not empty. It's not lacking anything. We do not fit the narrative, nor have I ever fit the narrative of the prosecution. I can only ask that you please read the many letters that come from those who know me, those who have lived with me, those who work next to me. Those are the ones who can speak of my character, my morals, my nature. You'll see that this is a stark contrast from who the prosecution claims that I am and who I've been.

"More than a decade ago I made the choice to work at the Bush Company. While working there I made poor choices. I never asked for anyone to be hurt. I worked there for under two years. I saved money to finance my education. I did not continue to work there. I went to school. I accepted gifts and money from men. I accepted gifts and money from Kent Leppink, but the prosecution would only have you focus on this three-month period of my relationship with Kent.

"The fact is I considered him a friend. My reaction upon hearing of his death was horrible. My reaction was genuine. It is true that later in anger I said things about him that were not kind. By that time I had learned things that I didn't know, and I shouldn't have said those things.

"The last decade should speak volumes about my character to you. I was defined as an ex-stripper. In fact, I've worked many different jobs prior to that, during that and after that. Excuse me. None of these jobs were mentioned. That job was actually a small part of my work history and an even smaller part of my being. None of these other jobs were put forth as a definition of me and my character by the prosecution, and this portrayal of me is not who I am. It only serves to fit them, because if they were to be honest about me it would not fit their theory.

Dead Man's Dancer 127

"I can only ask you to look at the letters, look at my life outside of the prosecution's attacks, look at what and who I am by my peers, my family, my friends, my neighbors. Those are the ones that can tell you. I ask you when sentencing me that you look at all of these. I beg you from the bottom of my heart to allow me the chance to go back to my family as soon as I possibly can.

"I know that you're bound by the verdict. I understand that. I try to understand what goes on, the process, and I think I have a good grasp of it. You sat here during the whole trial. You've seen everything, and I know that you're a separate entity from both of these tables, and I ask you to use that power and do what you can from your heart. Thank you."

In pronouncing his sentence, Judge Volland noted that Mechele had lived a good life for the last 10 years, and that she had a loving husband and a daughter, but she was able to live that life because she was getting away with murder. Kent Leppink had no such chance because he was deprived of those years by his murder.

Volland said he was convinced, based on the letters he had received about her and the evidence considered in the case, "there are in my judgment two Mechele Linehan's wrapped into one. One who ... was in fact seductive and manipulative in her behavior, and the other Mechele Linehan being someone who is supportive and caring, particularly to her daughter and her friends.

"It remains evident to me from that evidence and from those letters that people are clearly taken by Ms. Linehan's charm and remain so today, and the evidence at trial also convinces me that she used that same charm to a criminal design."

Volland said the death of Kent Leppink in a carefully plotted murder conspiracy, motivated by a large insurance policy, caused him to find that "it's the worst first-degree murder in its class."

"I'm bound by the jury's verdict," he said, "and my own conviction is Ms. Linehan played a principal role in this offense."

He said he could see no distinction "between the puppet who pulls the trigger and the puppeteer who pulls the strings, and in my judgment Ms. Linehan was the puppeteer who pulled the strings."

Since Volland had sentenced John Carlin to 99 years, he gave Mechele the same sentence. She would be eligible for parole after serving one third of the sentence, when she would be 68 years old.

CHAPTER 28
Spring Creek

Carlin's life at Spring Creek Correctional Center, a maximum-security men's prison in Seward, Alaska, was difficult from the beginning. He was reportedly a racist and often provoked arguments by high-handed actions like changing the television channel in a room full of prisoners watching their favorite show. He was severely beaten in September, 2007, by four Alaska Native inmates, a few months after he was sentenced at the end of his trial. A guard reported Carlin told him that he was lying on his bunk watching television when four men, one of whom had letters tattooed on his knuckles, "rolled in and beat him up." Donald Joseph, the only prisoner with tattoos on his knuckles was put in solitary confinement after the beating. Carlin was placed in protective custody, a section of the prison he described in a letter as similar to the primate section of a zoo.

Shortly after returning to the general prison population, he was attacked again. Fearing for his life, Carlin appealed to state officials and wrote a letter to Megan Holland at the Anchorage Daily News saying he needed to be moved or protected before the other prisoners killed him. He said his problem stemmed in part from visits he received from national television networks, which interviewed him for their programs on the case. He said the other prisoners were jealous of the attention and deference their famous fellow inmate was getting.

On October 27, 2008, Carlin was attacked a third time and beaten to death. The murder in Alaska's maximum-security prison was a rare one— the suspects were quickly identified by detectives—but the investigation dragged on for more than two years. Col. Audie Holloway, director of the Alaska State Troopers, said in May 2010 that his department had "dropped the ball" on the case. Perhaps because the investigators felt that the suspects were prisoners and weren't going anywhere, the crime lab review of DNA evidence was assigned a low priority and the case dragged on without arrests or announcements.

The investigation of Carlin's jailhouse beating death continued through 2010. Just before New Year's Day, 2011, the Alaska Department of Law reported that two of his fellow prisoners were indicted in Carlin's death. William N. Wassillie, 27, was charged with second-degree murder, burglary, and evidence tampering. Wassillie was already serving a 20-year sentence at Spring Creek for the brutal sexual assault of another prisoner while doing time at the state correctional facility in Bethel.

Indicted with him on similar charges was Tyler W. Heavyrunner, 29, who was serving a sentence at Spring Creek for raping a woman in 2005 and dumping her in a remote location outside Fairbanks. Heavyrunner had been scheduled for release in 2013 and Wassillie in 2021. The two men never went to trial; both accepted plea bargains and were sentenced to extra time on top of their existing sentences. Wassillie, who was apparently the central figure in the murderous attack, had 20 years added to his existing 20-year sentence. Heavyrunner received an additional year of prison time, but that sentence was suspended.

Carlin's son, John Carlin IV, sued the Alaska Department of Corrections for $500,000 because of his father's death. "I'm

Dead Man's Dancer

anxiously awaiting justice," he told a reporter. "I desperately want to finally find out what happened to my father."

The state settled the suit in early 2015 with a payment of $160,000 to the Estate of John Carlin III, presumably controlled by John Carlin IV, his son and closest relative.

Donald Joseph, the man sent to solitary the first time Carlin was beaten, added a complaint to a suit he had pending against the state. The amendment said prison officials didn't do enough to protect Carlin after the earlier beatings, one of which he participated in. Though the legal maneuver appeared to be a feigned protestation of innocence, it may have simply been a self-serving attempt to benefit from Carlin's death and perhaps win some monetary damages.

CHAPTER 29
The Appeal

After Mechele began her sentence at Alaska's only women's prison, Hiland Mountain Correctional Center in Eagle River, she busied herself by sewing prison uniforms and caring for abandoned dogs in a special program designed to rehabilitate both dogs and prisoners. Some of the animals went on to work as service dogs, offering inspiration and hope to the prisoners. Mechele also joined the Hiland Mountain Women's String Orchestra playing cello, an instrument she learned as a child.

The assignment sewing uniforms got her in trouble early on when Mechele modified a uniform shirt into a tank-top for herself, which did not sit well with the guards, many of them women who were unimpressed by Mechele's attraction for men. She was also found with a contraband pill, its nature not made public, and wandered into an off-limits area in the prison. The three infractions won her a stay in solitary confinement. Though she was initially scheduled to spend three months in the punishment section, she was returned to the general prison population after about 30 days.

Mechele sometimes didn't get along with her fellow prisoners—guards said she was too bossy—so she was put on a night-shift job to allow minimum interaction with others. She was in that situation, and getting along quite well, when her appeal was heard in December 2009.

To present her appeal, the family tapped its rapidly dwindling resources to retain two of Alaska's leading criminal defense attorneys, Jeff Feldman and Susan Orlansky. Feldman presented the case in a half-hour argument before a three-judge panel of the Alaska Court of Appeals on December 3, 2009.

His arguments were, in brief, that inflammatory and inappropriate testimony had been allowed about Mechele's occupation as a stripper, about the movie *The Last Seduction*, which was lavishly mentioned even though Judge Volland would not allow the jury to see the film itself, and in the condemnatory "letter from the grave" written by the victim. Feldman said the letter was improperly admitted and was effectively testimony by the victim, who could not be cross-examined because he was dead. It also named three people, who could not all have been the killers. Kent Leppink predicted that Mechele would be involved in his death, but the court could not with confidence assume that he was correct.

The Appeals Court ruled in February, 2010, that the movie—a critical part of arguments by prosecutor Pat Gullufsen—was unlike the Linehan case and had no apparent connection to the case. The judges said Kent's accusatory letter was inadmissible testimony and shouldn't have been used in any way. They ruled that the testimony about Mechele's two-year stripping career was acceptable since it revealed how she and the victim met and helped explain his infatuation with her. Since arguments about the movie were inappropriate, the prosecution was wrong to use the many references to the movie in presenting its case, including Gullufsen's emotionally powerful summation.

Mechele attended the proceeding in her yellow prison jumpsuit, her husband Colin waiting in the audience. Both were wearied by the years of litigation over the case and Mechele's two-and-a-half years behind bars. But, Feldman's arguments had given them reason to hope that the beginning of the end of their long nightmare was at hand.

The conviction was overturned, but Mechele was still under arrest and could not be free without posting bail. The family was then a million dollars in debt and unable to come up with the required $25,000 in money and property worth another $225,000. The cash was posted by a Pennsylvania businessman, Brian Watt—who had never met Mechele but was touched by her case—and the rest in property by an Anchorage man, Terry Stahlman, owner of a strip club and the city's Big Timber Hotel.

At the bail hearing, Judge Volland imposed severe restrictions on Mechele's movements, requiring that she stay in Anchorage and have 24-hour supervision by a court-approved custodian. He indicated she had ample motivation to comply with the restrictions on her movements, apparently a reference to the weaker nature of the state's remaining case. Banning the movie and Kent's inflammatory letter to his parents from use in the trial would make a new conviction difficult.

The bail restrictions proved to be virtual house arrest for both Mechele and her custodian, a woman she barely knew who was touched by her story. Mechele was allowed only two four-hour breaks away from the woman's home each week.[16] In July, Mechele was granted more lenient release conditions with no custodian, but she was still required to wear an electronic monitoring leg bracelet that could track her movements. She was required to remain within the Anchorage city limits and stay away from the airport and the homes and offices of several

---

16 The two breaks a week limit seemed harsh, but the rule was loosely enforced. During a meeting with Mechele, her husband and her daughter, Mechele told the author that nobody checked when or how long she was away from her custodian's home.

witnesses, but could otherwise move about freely.

Mechele rented an apartment and got a job as a receptionist at a hair salon, awaiting a new trial. That was scheduled tentatively[17] for the week of April 2, 2012, though the chance of a conviction without the inflammatory evidence items thrown out by the appeals court seemed fairly slim.

The April trial date became moot in December when Judge Volland ruled that the indictment should be thrown out since the improper and inflammatory evidence that caused the conviction to be thrown out was also used in the indictment. Mechele was granted her freedom for the first time since police came for her in Olympia five years earlier.

She made no statement but left the courtroom as quickly as she could. She and Colin brushed past waiting television cameramen, jumped into the elevator and were on a plane within a couple of hours, returning to Olympia.

Volland gave the prosecutors until Jan. 17 to decide if they would seek a new indictment based on the remaining evidence. When the date came, Assistant Attorney General Paul Miovas[18] told Superior Court Judge Larry Card[19] that his office was encountering a problem with the case since a key witness was unavailable.

Later he acknowledged that John Carlin IV, then 33, had retained a lawyer and, he was informed, if called to testify young Carlin would invoke his Fifth Amendment rights. The amendment mandates, among other things, that a person cannot be forced to testify against himself.

Carlin had talked freely to detectives who interviewed him

---

17 Trial dates are frequently changed to accommodate the schedules of lawyers and judges.

18 Miovas inherited the case when prosecutor Patrick Gullufsen retired the previous year.

19 Card was filling in for Judge Philip Volland on the case.

in Tacoma and testified about the case three times—before the grand jury and in the trials of his father and of Mechele. But, future testimony by him was suddenly unlikely.

In August, Miovas announced that the remaining evidence was insufficient to prove a case beyond a reasonable doubt, so Mechele would not be re-indicted. She and her family were free to begin rebuilding their lives.

CHAPTER 30
So Who Shot Kent Leppink?

The list of people who could have shot Kent Leppink is difficult to pin down. The possibilities include John Carlin III or perhaps young John Carlin IV and, of course, Mechele Linehan—or perhaps a fourth unknown party. Since the victim was shot by a Desert Eagle .44, a pistol rarely seen in Alaska and presumably the one purchased by the elder Carlin, it seems fairly certain that the killer had possession of the pistol and access to the Carlin hall closet both before and after the murder. But the weapon was never recovered. Since Kent's car was still in Anchorage and the keys in the pants pocket of his corpse, he obviously traveled to Hope in someone else's vehicle.

Kent had already written a letter mentioning the elder John Carlin as one who might murder him, so it seems unlikely that the prospective victim would willingly walk up a forest trail with Carlin walking behind, unless he was forced to walk at gunpoint.

Whether Mechele Linehan was involved in the murder of Kent Leppink—and in what way—is an intriguing question. The Cold Case Unit detectives who cracked the case followed professional procedures and closed a case that had nagged Alaska State Troopers for nearly a decade, but their ultimate conclusion that the killing resulted from a cold-blooded plot hatched by Mechele and carried out by her sometime fiancé John Carlin may or may not be an accurate reflection of what actually happened.

The officers were working from a body of evidence that started relatively small and grew as they developed the case, tracking down and interviewing the persons of interest, and using updated techniques to find and evaluate old materials. Detective Jim Stogsdill said they had the advantage of being assigned a case that was thoroughly investigated at the time of the murder, and which had comprehensive reports on the original detective work. But, they were necessarily looking through a limited window at an incident where much more was yet to be revealed. A hindsight look through about 5,000 pages of court testimony in two trials and the accumulated evidence suggests other possibilities for how the crime may have played out.

If the impression given by the email files recovered by computer forensic experts is accurate—and each piece has both a guilty explanation and an innocent explanation—then a reasonable person can still conclude that the young woman was the catalyst in a volatile situation that ran out of control and resulted in the death of Kent Leppink. She may or may not have known that the murder was in the works, may even have instigated it—but some of the email indicates she was having second thoughts, and perhaps panic attacks, about whatever she thought was coming.

Despite the trail leading to the older Carlin and Mechele, evidence in their two trials indicated there were a number of reasons to wonder whether the boy might indeed have been the actual shooter. Kent had been pressuring Carlin to tell him how to find the Hope cabin where Mechele was supposedly visiting, but Carlin said he refused. The son, however, could have told Kent that he knew where it was and driven him to the spot where Kent's body was found. Young Carlin was, in fact, the only one besides his father who credibly could have told Kent that he knew where the cabin was located—and been believed. Since Kent was convinced that the elder Carlin was plotting to kill him, Kent might have considered the son less of a threat and gone with him to search for the cabin and find Mechele and her lover. It seems unlikely that he would have gone to Hope with the elder Carlin and voluntarily walked up a forest trail with the man he suspected was trying to murder him walking along behind. Kent could have been forced to walk the trail at gunpoint, of course, so neither of the two Carlins could be ruled out as suspects on that basis.

One unexplained item that points to a younger suspect is the fact that testimony indicated young Carlin's fingerprints were on the gun, which led to his father's washing the pistol in bleach after the boy ran across it in the family hall closet. That means whoever used the pistol to kill Kent brought the weapon back to the house after the murder and returned it to the hall closet. That seems the act of a teenager who might worry less about police finding evidence remaining on the pistol and more about how his father might react when he noticed it missing. If an adult had used it, the gun would more likely have been buried in the forest or thrown into Cook Inlet.

Also unexplained is the statement by Scott Hilke during Mechele's trial that young Carlin told him on the day the household was notified of Kent's murder that Kent had been "gut-shot," information the boy should not have had.

It would also be reasonable to think that the elder John Carlin may have intended to kill Kent but—when the time came—was unable to go through with it. He was a tough man who sometimes threatened violence, but had not been known to actually commit any. There is a very real possibility that when the time came to carry out the murder he promised in bravado, Carlin simply chickened out. The question then becomes whether someone else stepped in, lured Kent to the road near Hope and shot him there—but there is no obvious answer. Since both Carlin and Kent are now dead, and young Carlin is invoking his right to refuse to testify, the truth of what really happened that day on the Hope Cutoff may never be known.

ABOUT THE AUTHOR

Tom Brennan is the author of *Murder at 40 Below*, *Cold Crime*, *The Snowflake Rebellion* and *Moose Dropping and Other Crimes Against Nature*. He lives in Anchorage.

www.ingramcontent.com/pod-product-compliance
Lightning Source LLC
Chambersburg PA
CBHW071715020426
42333CB00017B/2281